'Hollywood is a place where they'll pay a thousand dollars for your body and fifty cents for your soul . . .'

'I've slept with producers for work. I'd be a liar if I said I didn't . . .'

'All the girls did it. It was like part of the job. They wanted to sample the merchandise. If you didn't go along, there were another twenty-five girls who would. It wasn't any big tragedy.'
Marilyn Monroe

'The casting couch? There was only one of us ever made it to stardom without it – that was Bette Davis . . .'
Claudette Colbert

SELWYN FORD

The Casting Couch

GRAFTON BOOKS

A Division of the Collins Publishing Group

LONDON GLASGOW
TORONTO SYDNEY AUCKLAND

Grafton Books
A Division of the Collins Publishing Group
8 Grafton Street, London W1X 3LA

A Grafton UK Paperback Original 1990
Reprinted 1990

A CIP catalogue record for this book is available
from the British Library

ISBN 0-586-20386-9

Printed and bound in Great Britain by
Collins, Glasgow

Set in Times

The Author and Publishers wish to thank
the Kobal Collection for permission to
reproduce photographic material

Dedication

The people described in this book all achieved fame or notoriety in some way or another. They are the names we know and those that are remembered. Each and every one of them stands at the head of a legion of women – and men – who tried to imitate or emulate them and failed.

They were the ones for whom the dream was impossible from the outset, the ones for whom the long-awaited call never came. They were lied to, duped, took a wrong turning, leapt onto the wrong couch and still hung on, beyond reasonable expectations, still hoping. There never was, or is today, a waitress, a bartender or a car hop who doesn't harbour the dream. 'Classes' fill the empty day and feed the delusion that they are 'getting somewhere'.

Comes the day when they have to face the fact that the parade went by without them and all they have left are the memories of how they 'nearly' made it – the short list that was just one name too long and the part that 'should have been' theirs. They'll tell you as many lies as were ever told them, but they earned their lies in a hard school.

To that faceless, unknown army this book is dedicated.

Contents

	Introduction	9
1	Karno's Kasting Kapers	17
2	Celluloid into Gold – the New Alchemy	23
3	The Twenties – 'You Ain't Heard Nothing Yet'	48
4	Joan Crawford – A Star is Porn	73
5	The Thirties – 'We're in the Money'	82
6	Coast to Coast Casting Couch	114
7	Darryl F Zanuck – Mogul of the Thirties	122
8	The Forties – War and Witch-hunts	132
9	The Fifties – Invasion of the One-eyed Monsters	166
10	The Sixties – The Dinosaurs are Dying	190
11	The Long Killing of Marilyn	194
12	A Parade Gone By	213
	Epilogue	219
	Index	221

Introduction

The idea for this book began when a now celebrated actress told of her first encounter with the dreaded casting couch.

She was young, not yet even through drama school, when she managed to get seen by a prominent director. She read for him and obviously impressed him since she was called back for further reading three more times. These meetings were perfectly straightforward and completely professional and the belief grew in her that she really had a good chance of getting the promised role. It would be the kind of debut most young actresses dream about. Not only did the part run right through the picture but she would be playing opposite a distinguished British actor and was certain whoever played the role would generate a lot of interest. With each recall her hopes rose.

One side-effect of this interest was that she acquired an agent. One day he called her to tell her that she was prominent on the short list for the part and that he had arranged a meeting for her with the movie's producer. She gathered that if the producer approved her then the part was hers.

This particular producer had a reputation for 'couching' all his actresses with a particular liking for younger girls. In the three days between getting the call and the appointed hour our hopeful heroine was almost buried under an avalanche of warnings from well-meaning friends about what might be expected of her.

By the time she presented herself at her agent's office

her nerves were strung out clear across town but nevertheless she was determined that nothing was going to get
between her and the part.

Her mind seething with determination and terror in
equal parts she was finally admitted to the agent's office
where he sat with the producer.

'Well, darling,' the agent greeted her, 'if you'll take
your clothes off, you've got the part!'

Our heroine felt faint. This was it! Everything she had
been told was true. The 'couch' was right in front of her.

Steeling her failing nerves she turned away from the
unblinking eyes of the two men and hastily started removing her clothes. Turning back to face them she saw them
both staring at her open-mouthed. Inwardly she panicked.
Wasn't what they saw good enough? What else were they
expecting?

After a stunned silence which seemed, to her, to go on
forever her agent spoke as gently as he could. 'I *meant*,'
he said with careful emphasis, 'in the *movie*!'

The lady can now afford to tell this story against herself
with a laugh, but it does serve to illustrate how deeply the
casting couch has become ingrained in the show business
story.

Sex in exchange for career advancement was not
invented in Hollywood. It is the one tradition that cinema's older cousin, the theatre, handed down. In Hollywood, however, it became so much a part of everyday
life, so institutionalized, that 'colleges' sprang up to advise
new girls in town on the finer points of couch technique
along with specific advice about the likes and predilections
of certain executives with particular emphasis on any
variations from the norm that they might enjoy.
Obviously close proximity between beautiful young
ambitious girls and men with the power to grant them
their dreams would lead to thoughts of dalliance, but the

social framework of the Hollywood casting couch runs much deeper and is rooted in the almost accidental way in which the movie industry first grew up.

The cinema was the first mechanical means of mass entertainment. It had no roots, no traditions and demanded no inherited skills. Everything had to be invented or devised from the ground up. In many ways it paralleled the development of its contemporary, the aircraft industry. At first the 'experts' said it couldn't be done and even if it could be done there was no practical application for it. The smart money left it to enthusiasts, the practical men, to see the possibilities and work them out.

The cinema's closest relative – the live theatre – turned away in contempt at first sight of this new-born brat. They had good reason. The early movies robbed the stage actor of one of his most important assets – his voice. Then again the movies paid very badly. Professional actors and actresses would have nothing to do with it and so the first film makers had to learn how to get along without them. What they found was that all they needed was a pretty face and a capacity to convey a few basic emotions in mime. The first film makers found they could impart such rudimentary skills without too much effort and pretty faces were to be found everywhere. The investment needed to make one of the early one-reelers might be as low as $250 so no one was risking much if the girl they found behind the shop counter didn't work out. They learned that almost any girl could be transformed with a little attention to her hair and make-up, and brought in the first specialists to work on their charges – something the live theatre had never done. Following hard on their heels came 'drama' coaches to impart a little more skill to the silent mimes. This came to be known as the 'Studio System'.

Matching the indifference of the theatre establishment was that of the money men. They could see nothing in this medium but a fairground novelty. To them it was a nickel and dime business on a level with exhibiting bearded ladies and two-headed sheep. They left it to the fairground barkers and street traders to take up this 'toy' and develop its potential.

The early film makers were mostly immigrants, and being themselves only half-schooled in English, saw the immediate appeal of an entertainment that was cheap and told its stories in mainly visual terms. Within the darkness of the picture show these men provided a refuge from the strange and frightening country to which the immigrants had come in bewilderment and confusion. A simple story of an unhappy orphan or victim of society triumphing through to a happy ending was all the consolation and reassurance these audiences – who had probably never seen a live theatrical performance – demanded. Only someone who knew and had shared their fears could appreciate the impact such simple and naïve stories could have. The men with 'old' money, safe and secure in their own world were in no position to see how this new medium would grow. They left it to the 'nickel and dime' men until they, too late, realized how quickly those despised coins were mounting into thousands of the more superior dollars. By the time Wall Street started taking an interest the 'nickel and dime' men had made their own rules and created their own kingdoms complete with resources to match those who tried to take over.

The men who created the new industry and shaped it in their own image came to be known as the Moguls. Over the years these men acquired the image of small, fat, cigar-smoking cretins. They were the butt of many a joke about their half-educated solecisms and a street trader attitude that never quite matched their enormous wealth, power and influence. This image, much fostered in later years by college-educated writers who flushed guiltily at taking the large sums thrust on them by these same men, was only a partial truth and is largely the product of Hollywood's later years. In the beginning these men were young – little older than the century itself – but they came to know the business they created and first and foremost they knew their audience. In Europe there were already artists taking a serious interest in the new medium, but in the United States it was strictly a commercial business catering to a mass working class audience, largely immigrant. Their first heroines were sickly sweet girls whose virtue, ever in peril, was never surrendered. The huge successes of stars like Mary Pickford, Blanche Sweet, Bessie Love and many others, plus the realization that formal dramatic training was not a necessary prerequisite, brought a flood of aspirant girls to the courts of the early Moguls. These men, mainly young, remember, finding themselves newly enriched and now engulfed in an ocean of beautiful girls, all eager for their attentions and with little to offer other than themselves, would have been strange young men indeed if they had not responded.

So the Hollywood casting couch was born, destined to play a supporting role in countless thousands of personal and emotional dramas for more than fifty years. It was to become the most talked about and least written about aspect of the movies and establish itself so deeply in the story of Hollywood that as early as 1924 a pornographic film – then called a 'Stag Reel' – could be made entitled *The Casting Couch* which needed no explanation, beyond its title, as to plot and circumstances. A young girl enters an office where a cigar-smoking 'producer' rapidly seduces her. The girl responds enthusiastically and completes two acts of explicit sex in quick succession, ending in smiles all round and the signing of a contract. 'Ah,' the young lady starring in that stag reel must have thought, 'if only it were that simple.' In fact we do know something about that girl. She *did* go to Hollywood, and *did* apply exactly that approach to finding work during a career that lasted more than fifty years. The young lady starring in *The Casting Couch* was later known as Joan Crawford, of whom more later.

Our story will span those fifty years – from the start of the industry itself until the end of the Studio System and the death of the Moguls that devised and developed it. Why this arbitrary cut off? The answer, apart from our wish to avoid legal repercussions, is simply that when the Studio System ended with the flowering of the independent producer, the entire framework that supported the couch went with it. The movie studios shipped the couches over to their natural successors – the makers of television prime time soap operas – along with all other vestigial traces of the Studio System.

That is not to say that sex no longer plays a part in influencing a casting decision. What have changed are the stakes for which the participants are playing. Today's aspirant may seek to influence a casting decision just as her older sisters did, but today there are many differences in degree if not substance. In the early days of this century a girl that 'fell' was without honour, knew few means of contraception and could expect no pity or social support. The early casting couch was a place of peril on which a girl staked all. Today's changed values mean that the action is more likely to be extended into an 'affair' rather than a close encounter on an office couch. Today's hopeful will expect dinner or, at least, some semblance of social sparring. Her predecessors were lucky if they got to say 'hello'!

Curiously, the age of the casting couch dawned not on the sunny shores of California, nor even the bleaker blocks of New York, but in the grey drab streets of London's Kennington – the same streets that bred Charlie Chaplin. There stood the headquarters of a semi-literate man who became the most successful of England's many music hall impresarios – Fred Karno.

It was Karno who was to find local boy Charlie Chaplin and develop the urchin into the most famous of the early film comics, along with such other Hollywood greats as Stan Laurel. Karno himself thought nothing of the medium that was to kill his business, lure away his brightest talents and use, without acknowledgement, the visual style of comedy which he had developed. It might even be claimed that Karno's silent stage routines created the audience for the silent movie. Karno detested the 'new' movie medium and would have nothing to do with it, completely unaware that he was the one man in the world that understood it!

Karno even invented the casting couch tradition that so many of his graduates were to take with them to Hollywood. The story of Hollywood's casting couch would be incomplete without him.

1
Karno's Kasting Kapers

Fred Karno was the most prolific and successful music hall producer at the turn of the century. Practically illiterate, he got into show business with a troupe of travelling acrobats. The troupe made a sparse living from the country folk they entertained, but Karno developed a finely tuned athletic body that was capable of incredible feats. He soon split with the others of the troupe, called the Carnoes, and with a snip here and a snip there stole their name and so emerged as Fred Karno. Soon he graduated from tent performances to the regular music halls and discovered a talent for making people laugh. It was a completely visual style and developed quickly into what was to become known as slapstick. Karno created his own show and started touring it, gathering around him men like himself, nimble-limbed clowns. Business boomed, more troupes were formed as Karno stopped appearing personally and simply managed the shows.

Soon Karno was the richest and most successful music hall producer. He was also the most lecherous and sadistic. He married a young dancer from one of the early shows and it was as much due to her hard work – scrubbing down stages, building and painting props and generally breaking her back in the early days – that Karno's empire grew as it did. In return he treated her like a dependent slave. Keeping her short of money, flaunting his sexual conquests of the girls in his employ, he didn't bother coming home most weeks and when he did usually it was to beat her up for some supposed misdemeanour.

Fred Karno operated a system of *droit de seigneur* over every female employee that would have shamed a feudal lord. If there was anything to be said in favour of this sadistic bully boy then it was that he made no attempt to hide from anyone the fact that any girl wanting to work in any of his shows had first to grace his couch – not only then but at any time in the future when the mood took him. Karno's attitude was that once a girl signed a contract with him then he owned her, not just the use of her talents, but her body too. His wrath could create stinging humiliation. Harriet Morrison was one young dancer that got the full treatment when Karno found out that she had sneaked off between performances at the Camberwell Palace and got married. That evening, as she was showing her new ring to the other girls, she got a summons to report immediately to the fun palace, Karno's Kennington headquarters.

Arriving there she found an angry Karno demanding to know the reason for her 'betrayal' of him. Confused, Harriet was starting to ask what he meant when he started hitting her. He knocked her to the ground ripped off her clothes and raped her and then threw her out on the street. Harriet couldn't face returning to her new husband and instead took herself to the Thames where her body floated up some three days later. Karno was later to deny that she had ever arrived at his headquarters, where, according to him, she had been summoned so that he could 'congratulate' her.

Among the effects which Karno returned to her groom were several pornographic pictures of Harriet taken with Karno. Karno had a penchant for explicit photographs taken of his various misdeeds. They were to figure largely in the divorce case which his long-suffering wife was finally convinced to bring. She was reluctant to let her lawyer use the photographs, which Karno had sent her

over the years, with inscriptions such as, 'See, she'll do
all those things you won't do!' Karno lied throughout the
hearing, and turned up one night at his wife's mean little
Brixton home and, getting her drunk, slept with her,
afterwards triumphantly announcing the fact to the world
and claiming that it showed she had acquiesced in whatever misdeeds she claimed he had done. It looked as if
Karno had finally triumphed, until, finally and tearfully,
she gave permission for the pornographic pictures to be
produced.

Karno's defence collapsed and his wife was awarded
ten pounds a week – a princely sum in those days, or
would have been had he, one of the richest of men, ever
paid it.

If Karno could so treat his legal wife we can fairly
deduce what his attitude to those aspirant young enter-
tainers that dared cross his office threshold would be. But
we do not have to surmise since we have three eye-witness
reports – naturally from women who resisted.

Elsie Manners was seventeen years old in 1911 when
she turned up in Kennington for her appointment with
Karno. She was a very beautiful natural blonde with the
then fashionable hour glass figure. Karno's type to a tee.
Elsie tells the story of what happened. 'I got there as
instructed at twelve-thirty. I was shaking with nerves
because I knew Mr Karno's reputation but somehow
hoped that it wouldn't happen to me! His male secretary
showed me into his office and, as he was closing the door,
was told to go to lunch.

' "Take your coat off and sit down," Mr Karno told me.
Mr Karno hardly looked at me and continued reading
some papers on his desk. Finally he pulled a large piece
of paper towards him and started rattling off questions.
Name . . . age . . . height . . .

'I was five foot seven, which was very tall for those days.

'"Good," said Mr Karno. "I like tall girls. Chest, waist, hips?"

'Feeling as if I was at the dressmaker's I told him, and he, still not looking at me, told me to stand up and walk round the room. I did that and then he told me to come and stand in front of him. When I did he started unbuttoning my blouse. I pushed his hands away but he persisted.

'"If I hire a thirty-six inch bust I want to know if it's what I'm paying for!" he told me.

'I just stood there until he had unbuttoned my blouse completely. My brain was screaming at me to do something but somehow I couldn't. I was paralysed. Mr Karno looked at my breasts and grudgingly admitted they could be the thirty-six inches I'd claimed.

'"Right," he said. "There's two jobs. One stands in at two pounds a week the other at four. Which do you want?"

'Naturally I stuttered that I wanted the four.

'"Right," said Mr Karno, "get the rest of your clothes off, get on the couch and we'll see if you're worth four quid . . ."'

Panic broke her paralysis and Elsie grabbed up her clothes and ran out of the office. Karno's laugh pursued her down the corridor. 'Stupid cow!' he shouted after her. 'Think I'm going to chase you? I got dozens like you coming in every day!'

That was Karno at the height of his fame and wealth. He was in very different circumstances some twenty years later when he was casting a show called *Laffs* for the London Palladium. A young would-be singer called Phyllis Dixey came to see him. Phyllis was in later years to become famous as Britain's answer to Gypsy Rose Lee, performing a similar coy strip act, but in those days she had yet to take off her clothes in public.

In the twenty-year interval since Elsie Manners had met Karno nothing had changed. Fred eventually looked up at the pretty young blonde and his first question was, 'Natural blonde? Collar and cuffs match, do they? Figure's all right from what I can see of it. You wearing a girdle?'

Karno was up on his feet and pushing and prodding at Phyllis as if seeking the answer to his questions by braille.

Phyllis stood her ground as best she could. 'I came here to be auditioned as a singer,' she told him, 'not to be pawed!'

Karno grinned. 'No need for the audition,' he told her. 'You've got the part!'

He handed her a standard contract form and a pen. As she leaned over to sign it she felt his hand race up her skirt, and he thrust her forward over the desk. Phyllis managed to jab Karno's hand with the pen and as he slumped into a chair sucking on his damaged hand she smiled sweetly and left his office.

Afterwards she would tell the story with the tag, 'I failed my first audition. I couldn't sing in the horizontal position.'

There are legions of such stories among the veterans of the Karno Kouch. Despite his lechery there is no doubt that Karno was a visual comedy genius. He discovered and developed many talents that were to become famous and a couple that were to become legends – Chaplin and Stan Laurel among them. It was while they were playing in a Karno show touring the United States that both Chaplin and Laurel got Hollywood offers. In those days of the silents Karno's comic style was exactly what Hollywood wanted. It was surely no coincidence that Mack

Sennett called his comedy troupe the Keystone Kops, obviously borrowing the 'K' from Karno.

Fred Karno was music hall's gift to those early one-reelers and Chaplin and Laurel made liberal use of material that had first been developed by Karno.

Curiously, Karno himself never got into the medium to which he contributed so much. Instead his social ambitions and overweening ego caused him to sink his vast fortune into a weekend roadhouse on Tagg's Island in the Thames which he, naturally, named Karno's Karsino. He had a glittering few weeks when he was lavishly handing out freebies to all and sundry, but soon the crowds diminished and instead of the classy weekend establishment for the rich he found himself running a picnic ground for day trippers whose tastes ran more to beer than champagne.

Almost ruined, Karno tried trawling his meagre stock of friends for jobs, finally coming out to Hollywood in the twenties and getting some hand-out work from Hal Roach who as a producer was, at this time, second only to Sennett in fame. For Karno it was just a taste of the humiliation he had heaped on others throughout his career.

But Karno had bequeathed not only his comic style to the nascent movie industry but also his casting couch mores. Sennett, Chaplin and others had learned much from him and ensured that the spirit of Karno pursued all those aspiring young girls that were about to descend in droves on Hollywood. They would never have heard of Karno, certainly not of Harriet Morrison or Elsie Manners, but they were soon to find themselves travelling the same road and learning the meaning of the Hollywood Handshake.

2
Celluloid into Gold – the New Alchemy

Thomas Edison formed the very first 'film manufacturing company' in 1897. He had obtained a US patent on the cinematographic camera and projection systems. Edison wasn't alone in this invention. Similar apparatus had independently been made in both Britain and France. Edison ignored them. He considered that his US patent gave him the sole right not only to the equipment but also the films that could now be made by it. He soon extended his thinking to cover the entire business and set about defending his rights with avalanches of law suits and, when he felt that too slow a process, sent in gangs of bully boys to smash up the studios and equipment of maverick film makers who were outside his privileged, licensed companies. He formed these licensed companies into the Motion Picture Patents Company which was immediately dubbed 'the Trust'. Edison's own company, Vitagraph, was joined by other production companies such as Selig, Kalem, Pathé, Melies, Lubin and Essanay. They felt ever-threatened by the many, mostly transient, companies that were set up to make 'bootleg' pictures. The pictures they were making were rarely more than ten minutes long, and while the Trust companies centred themselves in New York and Chicago the outsider 'pirate' companies were harassed into finding alternative locations where the Trust lawyers and wrecking crews couldn't find them. They tried Florida and Cuba, and all points west until, coming to the Pacific Ocean, they found what they were looking for. Varied landscapes, beaches and mountains, but most of all sunshine. In those pre-smog days the beaches and hills around Los Angeles enjoyed crystal-clear sun for most days of the year and the early film stock demanded strong light; even interiors were photographed by the light of the sun.

While it was the maverick independents who were to come in droves to colonize this picture-making paradise it was, curiously enough, one of the insider Trust companies that found it. In 1907 Colonel William Selig found the bad weather in Chicago seriously holding up production. He needed some beach scenes to complete *The Count of Monte Cristo* and, tiring of the extended absence of the sun, packed his director, cameraman and cast on to a train with orders to keep going west until they found some sunshine. They found it on the beach at Santa Monica a few short miles from a sleepy little village called Hollywood. Little did its residents know what was about to hit them!

The sunshine of Santa Monica faded from the minds of the Selig company until in 1909 the weather again closed in and stopped production. Colonel Selig again sent a company southwest. The same director, Francis Boggs, brought with him the crew and actors for *Heart of a Race Riot*, shot in a rented Chinese laundry in downtown Los Angeles. So pleased was Selig with the uninterrupted shooting schedules possible in California that he moved there on a more permanent basis and set up shop in Edendale. Others soon followed, but the first in Hollywood itself was the Nestor company which took over a recently closed brothel and turned it into a studio.

The average total cost of the one-reelers of the day was about a thousand dollars. This was in no small part due to the low pay which the screen actors received. Leading players would be hired, just like any other studio employee, on a weekly basis and might expect as much as $25 a week. These leading players were not billed.

Nobody knew their names and it was left to the movie-going public to come up with names for them – The Vitagraph Girl, The Biograph Girl, Essanay's Latin Lover; these, and others less flattering, were hung about the necks of the anonymous players and so the public's favourites were acknowledged.

One exhibitor who noticed that his box office take rose whenever he had a movie by the anonymous Biograph Girl, was one Carl G Laemmle. He saw the money being made by the thousand dollar one reelers and decided to get into manufacturing for himself. Forming the Universal Film Manufacturing Company, he started looking for a star. His eye fell upon one Florence Lawrence – then the reigning Biograph Girl. Having established that the tiny Miss Lawrence had a salary to match – $25 a week for making an average of four one-reelers – Laemmle travelled to Chicago and set about meeting her. Miss Lawrence went to his hotel suite where she was astonished to find herself being offered a rise in pay from $25 to $1,000 a week. She went into shock and Laemmle realized he had a problem. Miss Lawrence, delectable and widely known, had no name of her own. She was The Biograph Girl, and it dawned on Laemmle that by leaving that company she would also leave her public identity behind.

Laemmle thought hard and long and came up with the movie world's first publicity stunt. First he moved the willing Miss Lawrence into his hotel and carefully 'disappeared' her. News that The Biograph Girl was missing made a small item in a couple of papers. Laemmle needed more. He called these papers and the news agencies and informed them that the reason The Biograph Girl was missing was because she had been knocked down and killed by a streetcar. He didn't forget to add that her real name was Florence Lawrence. The papers splashed the story with big headlines: 'FLORENCE LAWRENCE, THE BIO-GRAPH GIRL, KILLED IN STREETCAR ACCIDENT'. The nation was barely into mourning before an 'indignant' Laemmle was on the phone protesting that this was all a phony story put out by Biograph to cover the fact that Florence Lawrence had changed companies and was now under contract to the Universal Film Manufacturing Company and – and this was the news that was to change the whole nature of the nascent movie industry – she was being paid the astronomical sum of $1,000 a week!

While the nation's moviegoers sighed a collective sigh of relief that their favourite was still alive and working, the movie industry went into uproar. Soon Florence's replacement at Biograph, Mary Pickford, and fellow anonymous star Mabel Normand were demanding billing and salaries to match. The studios for the first time acknowledged the power of their players and, not without a fight, caved in. So the star system began.

The results were astonishing. Mary Pickford had been given $1,000 a week right off, but she continued testing her powers and there was only the merest pause before she was earning $2,000 and then $10,000 a week payable in cash each Monday morning before the start of work! Charles Chaplin – fired by Sennett – was taken on by Mutual. He got $10,000 a week and a signing-on bonus of $150,000.

Carl G Laemmle had opened the floodgates and the leading players went down under an avalanche of dollars. These sums, welcome even today, were unheard of in the days before the First World War. The public looked in awe at people who commanded such riches and concluded they must be demi-gods. The ex-'players', now movie stars rich as Croesus, responded by playing up the image the public had laid on them, and all across America mothers eyed their prettiest daughters speculatively.

Those with settled families usually found it was their fathers that blocked any such move. They had been born before the turn of the century, an era when 'ladies' wore whalebone corsets and dresses that also served to sweep the streets clean. Those mothers who were widowed, divorced or in some way separated from the restraining hand of a Victorian father had no such inhibitions. This probably accounts for the incredibly high proportion of future stars who came from broken homes. They included such names as Dorothy and Lilian Gish, Anna Sten, Mary Pickford, Joan Crawford, Betty Hutton, Myrna Loy, Pola Negri, Merle Oberon, Margaret O'Brien, Barbara Stanwyck, Carole Lombard, Ginger Rogers, Norma Shearer, Lana Turner, Loretta Young, Ruth Chatterton, Olivia de Havilland and her sister Joan Fontaine, Kay Francis, Paulette Goddard, Jean Harlow, Miriam Hopkins, Bette Davis and Marilyn Monroe. The list could go on and on, but there are sufficient here to make the point.

The earliest of these stars usually came to Hollywood escorted by their mothers. They had to be. Most of them were less than sixteen years old. The reason for this was technical. Back in those early days the only form of lighting that could render a clear image on the slow stock was bright sunlight. Any woman with even the slightest blemish or faintest age lines would photograph like an aged crone. The result was a flood of twelve- and thirteen-year-olds playing mature womanly roles as wives, mistresses and even vamps. The fact that these girls started so young continues to surprise even today; Gloria Swanson was able to play mature roles before the First World War and still be around to make an appearance in *Airport '75*. At an age when most of today's would-be actresses are graduating from drama school, Gloria had already starred in some fifty movies. Others started even younger. Bebe Daniels played adult roles at thirteen. Lilian and

Dorothy Gish were fourteen and fifteen respectively when they starred. Mary Pickford was fourteen. It was an attitude which was going to be a long time changing. As late as 1930 a full-page article appeared in a family fan magazine called *Picture Show*. The subject was a very youthful Loretta Young. Accompanied by a discreet semi-nude photograph the article, worth quoting in full, read:

SOPHISTICATED SIXTEEN

To be earning at fifteen a salary that most of us would not despise annually; to be known and admired by thousands all over the world; and to take it all as a matter of course could only happen in the glamorous magic world of film. It has happened to Loretta Young.

When she left the convent, where she had been educated, her sisters Sally Blane and Polly Ann Young were already at the job in which all three had worked as tiny children. One of Polly's jobs overlapped another, so she asked Loretta to double for her. Loretta did, for the first day. The second day she was offered a contract on her own account.

Was Loretta wrought up about it? Not a bit. She just accepted it as if it were her due, with a composure that is the keynote of her character. For this sixteen-year-old child has the maturity and poise of twenty-six. Polished, pointed, manicured nails; high-heeled shoes, thin silk stockings, skilfully carmined lips, an outlook that has nothing childish in it except the assumption that thirty is dreadfully old – this is Loretta.

She visited her first night club at the age of thirteen. She wore evening dress and went alone with a man.

Childish pleasures and games Loretta can scarcely remember. It is the penalty of being a child actress and a leading lady, simulating a woman's emotions at fifteen; although Loretta seems to harbour no regrets, but rather to accept it as inevitable and natural. She explains that all the High School boys and girls she had known were as sophisticated as herself – that is the modern youth.

A teacher attends Loretta three hours daily, tutoring while she is at the studio, for legally this worldly-wise Loretta is still a child. Legally, perhaps, but legally only.

This newscutting, despite belonging to 1930, typifies the attitudes to the child/woman actress prevailing in Hollywood earlier in the century. This was a studio press release published in a family magazine. Any studio publicist putting out stories on night-clubbing thirteen-year-old contract artistes in this 'liberated' era would face instant firing. It was stories like this that encouraged mothers to bring their daughters west and, often, directly to the couch.

Times were hard for a widowed or divorced mother. A maintenance order served in one county would have no effect if the erring father moved to a different one. In desperation many saw their daughters' good looks as the only way out. In Hollywood they found a community, newly rich and hardly daring to believe it was going to last, throwing what seemed to be a permanent party. The new arrivals looked around bewildered, feeling themselves several drinks behind; they had to hurry to catch up. Desperation can do strange things to mothers of young girls and many of them provided the 'wise' counsel that pushed so many of their daughters towards the couch.

One of the most notorious starting points for a girl whose only asset was her looks was with Mack Sennett's Bathing Beauties. Here the comedy stars like Chaplin, Stan Laurel, Chester Conklin, Ben Turpin and many others were dragging unbelievable riches to Sennett. The girls of the Bathing Beauty line-up were there solely to provide a decorative background while the real money was made out front. The ex-vaudevillians that Sennett had recruited brought with them the old music hall attitude towards the chorus line; the top comic got first pick and so on down the line. It was said that many of them kept 'race cards' on the girls and ticked them off as they scored. Mack Sennett himself didn't need to keep a card. No girl even got on the lot who hadn't first been on his casting couch. Established early, Sennett's was probably the archetypal couch; setting the tradition that so many others were to follow. Frenetic though his comedy was, Sennett nevertheless was a genuine pioneer film maker and is credited with adapting to the screen the stage routines inherited from such people as Karno. Many other innovations credited to others can be first seen in Sennett's crazy comedies. Many of those Bathing Beauties that he first used went on to become the first big stars of the screen: Ruth Rich, Gloria Swanson, Mabel Normand, the Talmadge sisters, Juanita Hansen, and Alma Rubens.

One of the biggest stars of this decade – and no other – was also the exception. Theda Bara was exceptional in many ways. She was twenty-four when she made her first movie. The picture was made in 1914 and called *A Fool There Was*, based on a Rudyard Kipling poem, 'The Vampire'. Vampire was shortened to 'vamp', and became the generic name for all screen ladies with a winning way with men. Theda was the first of many to bear the title. A complete contrast to the simpering virgins then reigning as movie queens, Theda was an immediate success. The modest little picture took off and laid the foundation of the fortune of its producer, William Fox, who immediately started pouring out ludicrous 'biographies' of his new star. Her name, someone spotted, was an anagram of Arab Death, so she was allotted a birthplace in 'the shadow of the Sphinx', which meant that the Sphinx's shadow must have reached Cincinnati, Ohio, since that was where Theodosia Goodman was born in 1890. Such nonsensical publicity obscured her real origins and so not much is known of what Theodosia was doing for the first twenty-two years of her life. The generally accepted version is that she was trying to make the grade as a stage actress but failed. In or about 1912 she started being seen around the East Coast movie studios, usually as someone's 'date'. A director named Frank Powell took a liking to her and when he was assigned *A Fool There Was* put her, against vociferous opposition, into the lead. Any time she tried to play anything other than a man-hungry home wrecker – such as Juliet – the public turned its back on her. She was therefore kept strictly to parts that enhanced her 'evil' image and the result was that after the First World War, when the public began to accept that you didn't have to be 'exotic' or 'foreign' to be a bad girl, her style and acting – such as it was – seemed hopelessly old-fashioned and out of date. Theda faded fast, but in her passing she spawned a new fashion and many imitators quickly formed up behind her.

The acceptance of stars such as Theda soon led to other producers becoming even more daring. The full-frontal nude made her first appearance on the Hollywood screen in 1916, in the delectable shape of Olympic swimming star Annette Kellerman. The hicks drooled, and other appearances followed, opening the way for Audrey Munson to be naked in *Purity*. Miss Munson had come to Hollywood, hailed as the girl with the perfect body, after being chosen as the model for the medals issued at the San Francisco World's Fair. Munson and Kellerman might be considered as 'gimmick' nudes, but nudity crept into dramatic features. After rape and pillage in *Birth of a Nation* – D W Griffith's epic paean of praise for the Ku-Klux-Klan – he went on to make *Intolerance*. This film was made partly to allay the outcry there had been over *Nation*. It is a loose and badly constructed lope through history, contrasting modern-day ethics with those of the past, with many a stop-off at orgies and riotous banquets along the way. It didn't work. Where *Birth of a Nation* had been shot for the excessive budget of over $200,000 and then brought back the even more incredible sum of

$22 *million* – worth, perhaps, as many hundreds of millions today – *Intolerance* was made at a cost of $445,000 and failed to bring back even its production costs. There were many reasons for this. Public antipathy to the overt racialism of its director, the entry of the US into the First World War and the excessive costs of distribution. D W Griffith, the magic money-maker, was in a position, prior to *Intolerance*, to dictate his terms. He insisted on roadshowing the movie as if it were a live theatre piece, and also that every performance be accompanied by a full orchestra. Costs ate up any meagre profit there might have been. Hollywood forgot the *Birth of a Nation* money mill and consigned Griffith to the has-been list and he never again was able to scale the heights of his earliest efforts. Griffith was the discoverer of many of the girl children/leading ladies of the teen years – among them Lilian and Dorothy Gish, Bessie Love and Blanche Sweet – all of whom came under his tutelage as thirteen- to fifteen-year-olds. D W Griffith had started out in the New York Biograph studios and brought with him a habit of testing out his leading ladies on the casting couch. Along with his right-wing views he had a taste for applying the whip. It was this mutuality of interest that brought Erich von Stroheim from extra to Griffith's assistant. Von Stroheim picked up on gossip about Griffith's peculiar pleasures and started introducing him to willing young ladies whom he had previously tested. Griffith recognized the nascent talent in von Stroheim and they became very close. It was von Stroheim who would arrange party calls for the girls under contract to Griffith and supervise the resulting orgies. Von Stroheim, in later years, put many of these orgies on film – though they never reached the public screen – in such movies as *The Merry Widow*, *Wedding March*, *The Honeymoon* and *Queen Kelly*, in which he employed many of the veterans of his household orgies to re-create on screen what they had previously performed in semi-privacy. Much of the footage von Stroheim shot behind closed studio doors has never seen the light of a projector and was rumoured destroyed for fear of prosecution if it ever slipped the tight security of the studio vaults. Von Stroheim was profligate with other people's money and shot pictures of inordinate length for those days, sometimes running to eleven reels when six were considered more than enough. Von Stroheim managed to bring true depth and perspective to his characters, and while the movies he *shot* would have been sensational, the mutilated versions that were *shown* were just tame and boring to the audiences. Few of his movies made money and people wondered why he was constantly funded by producers not noted for their patience. What the outside world didn't know about was the pulling power of Stroheim's parties.

Having graduated from the schools of Fred Karno *and* Mack Sennett it should be no surprise that Charles Chaplin brought with him a taste for casting on the couch. His particular distinction, however, was for creating scandal with scandalously young girls. This was a fetish that was to haunt him all his life and cause endless trouble. It seems strange that Chaplin should be so often reviled for doing what everybody else was doing, while others got away with it. Part of the answer lay in the enmity of other producers. Chaplin had enjoyed a meteoric rise from banana-skin comedian to stratospherically salaried employee and had then broken from the Moguls and become the first star to form his own independent production company. As they were to do with Lewis Selznick, the Moguls lay in wait for the first scandal. His earliest casting successes were ex-Sennett comedians like Mabel Normand and Edna Purviance. Chaplin worked hard and found life between pictures unendurable. Those hours he filled with chasing that which he called 'the most beautiful form of human life – the very young girl just starting to bloom'. Whereas Edna Purviance and Mabel Normand hardly fitted this idyllic picture two other young ladies came into his life at about the same time. The first was Mildred Harris. She was thirteen when she caught Chaplin's eye. Mildred dreamed of a career in pictures – which she got – while her mother dreamed of marrying her off to the rich young Chaplin – he was twenty-five. Unknown to both of them Chaplin had already picked out Mildred's successor – a gorgeous little girl called Lita Grey. Unfortunately, in 1916 she was only six years old and so even Chaplin was forced to put her in the pending tray.

Meanwhile little Mildred attended Chaplin's studio for intensive coaching. Chaplin, when stuck for an idea, would retire from the set, picking up Mildred or a passing extra, and have them perform fellatio while he consulted the Muse. It was Mildred's mother who suggested that such activities were not going to lead to the desired result. She explained the deeper mysteries of the man/woman relationship and a wide-eyed Mildred set about accommodating herself and Chaplin. Mildred reported that things were now moving in the right direction and Mother waited an impatient two months before storming in on Chaplin and reporting that her daughter was in a delicate condition. Chaplin, fearing charges of statutory rape, did the only thing Mother would allow and married the child. It was only afterwards that he discovered that little Mildred had been 'mistaken' and wasn't pregnant after all. Chaplin, while noting that his wife was no mental giant, was nevertheless enchanted with the new freedom of the marriage bed. There were, however, two clouds on this prospect of married bliss. The first was Louis B Mayer. He signed the new Mrs Charles Chaplin to a contract, something Chaplin had overlooked, and started out to make pictures billing her in her newly acquired married name. Charles was furious, and it led to a famous knockdown fight in the foyer of the Alexandria Hotel when Chaplin accused Mayer of interfering in his marriage and incautiously invited the tiny but tough executive to 'step outside'. Mayer, whose muscles had been toned working as a scrap dealer, didn't bother with the walk. He put a fist into Charlie's face there and then. Charlie went flying across the foyer and cannoned into a mirror which broke. The Alexandria sent the bill for the cracked mirror to Chaplin. Chaplin sent it to Mayer, and Mayer sent it back to Chaplin. This exchange went on for over a year until one or other tired of the game and settled it. Cloud one, round one. Knockout.

The other cloud was that little Mildred developed a marked distaste for men. Charlie found out she was seeing Alla Nazimova – leader of the movies' lesbian circle – and coming home quite flushed of face. Enter the lawyers and exit Mildred. It was 1920 and little Lita Grey was now twelve years old and coming along nicely. She was taken under contract and studied diligently under the master even though, at this age, his plans for her remained under wraps. Given that Chaplin's doings with little Mildred were common knowledge, Lita's mother must have been incredibly naïve or wilfully negligent to have given Chaplin so much rein with her tiny girl child. She couldn't have failed to notice the heavy traffic in girl starlets passing into Chaplin's inner sanctum and emerging triumphantly ten minutes later.

Those that sinned in those early days were indeed fortunate. The compliant press happily smoothed down the rougher edges of this and many other episodes and Chaplin's popularity hardly wavered. There were already fan magazines but they did not yet deal in scandal. The many indiscretions of the stars in Hollywood were kept quiet, the newspapers and journalists seeing profit in keeping the mythology alive: the 'retainers' they received from the studios didn't hurt.

It helped to have an affair with a high-powered newspaper magnate. Marion Davies found such a protector in William Randolph Hearst and their liaison lasted for thirty-five years.

Florenz Ziegfeld had established a Broadway reputation for shows that 'glorified the American Girl'. His off-stage reputation was that of a relentless pursuer of young girls, and none that worked for him escaped the compulsory couch he kept in his office. Ziegfeld's passion was to provide many a girl – they got too old at seventeen – for Hollywood, where they would arrive with a clear understanding of the couch and its benefits. One of the stellar graduates of the Ziegfeld couch was Marion Davies, who danced in the chorus line from the age of fourteen. Like all other Ziegfeld chorines she was wined and dined by the ageing stage door Johnnies. Bunches of roses would, like as not, have a hundred-dollar bill concealed in their delicate folds. Diamond watches and bracelets were also to be found among the tender blossoms. A girl on receiving such a tribute could either accept or reject the implied offer. Such an offering would be followed by a viewing of prospects at parties given for that express purpose. One such popular meeting place was the salon of Broadway musical star Elsie Janis. There Miss Janis would play mix and match among the tycoons and the showgirls. Marion, who suffered from a severe stammer, was with one Paul Block when she first met Hearst. Both were newspaper proprietors and Hearst looked jealously on at Block's nubile young 'friend'. Hearst was fifty-two, Marion seventeen when he introduced himself by crushing a Tiffany watch in her surprised little hand. Marion promptly lost it. Janis informed Hearst of the tragedy and Hearst delivered a replacement. Marion was impressed. It was while she was in Florida with yet another admirer, Jim Deering, that she next came across Hearst. His Cadillac was pointed out to her while she was out cycling. Marion promptly rode into the side of it and engineered an accident. Hearst leapt from the offending vehicle and rushed towards Marion as she lay sprawled indecently on the ground. Having checked that no bones were broken he then seemed to be pretending not to know her. Marion was puzzled until she noticed that his wife, an ageing thirty-three, was accompanying her husband. However, the 'accident' had provided the necessary signal to Hearst that a further approach to Marion might meet with success. There followed many telephone calls to the Deering residence from Hearst using various names, and as a consequence Marion stole several hours away from her current admirer to set up the new one.

Hearst was smitten. Calculating Marion less so. Hearst was a jealous man. Tired of being passed around the Broadway inner circle she saw Hearst as a candidate for marriage. Her problem was that if she turned away all other admirers on those occasions when Hearst was tending business elsewhere, and then he didn't come through as an ardent husband, she would have burned her boats. On the other hand if she continued to see other men it was almost certain that Hearst wouldn't marry her. Marion was too young to know that Hearst would have no intention of marrying her. Neither could she know that their relationship would last thirty-five years. While Hearst openly acknowledged her and, throughout those long years, remained faithful to her, Marion repaid him with outside affairs and deceptions throughout their relationship.

She continued to hope that Hearst would marry her but

settled for the next best thing – movie stardom. Opportunities on Broadway were limited for Marion. Her stammer barred her from ever rising out of the chorus and by the standards of the day she was, at seventeen, getting long in the tooth. The movies of the day, being silent, beckoned her like a saviour.

Hearst financed her first modest essay into the genre: a production of a story she had written called *Runaway Romany*, starring herself. The picture opened to weak reviews and even weaker takings, a pattern which, with a few honourable exceptions, was to be the norm for her entire career. Hearst tried her again, this time with prolonged exposure in a thirty-episode serial in the manner of *Perils of Pauline*, Marion's effort being called *Betty Fairfax*. Only the newspapers controlled by Hearst loved it. Everyone else hated it. Hearst put out an order that his papers should print at least one story or photograph of Marion at least once a week. They were all adulatory. Hearst's fortune was to continue pouring down on Marion for forty-six movies until even the Hearst money ran out. Marion repaid him by continuing to enjoy as many affairs as Hollywood could provide.

But for the grace of God Marion might have found herself in the hands of someone far less benevolent than Hearst since, about the time she was seeking an outlet for talents that didn't require a speaking voice, another movie mogul was at the zenith of his powers, Lewis Selznick. If ever there was an opportunist on Broadway it was Lewis J. He first saw opportunity beckon when his jewellery business failed. Among the meagre ranks of Selznick's friends was one Dintenfass. Selznick went to him hoping for a stake to get started again or, as a last resort, a job. Selznick had a wife and two growing sons to support. Dintenfass didn't have anything immediate but promised to look out for Lewis J. Just as their meeting was about to end Dintenfass started telling Selznick about an unhappy investment he had rashly made. He had put money into Universal, the company formed up by Carl G Laemmle and a huge Irishman called Pat Powers. It had seemed like a good idea at the time but now Dintenfass was sure the company was headed for bankruptcy since the two partners were fighting each other with such intensity that they were no longer speaking to each other. Dintenfass wanted to sell out his share but neither partner was willing to buy. Selznick, for want of anything else to do, offered to negotiate on Dintenfass' behalf.

Selznick went to the Universal offices on Broadway and saw that things were even worse than he feared. Universal was split into two warring camps by the feud, each partner operating what amounted to a separate business. Selznick went first to Pat Powers but met with a frosty 'no'. Nothing daunted he next tried Laemmle, adjusting his sales pitch to point out that whoever bought Dintenfass' share would have control. Laemmle bought.

For anyone less desperate than Selznick this might have been the end of the story – shareholding sold, commission earned. For Selznick a company whose two partners were not speaking to each other, and which was paralysed into near total inaction, presented an opportunity. Noting that the company had no general manager, and spotting an empty office, Selznick appointed himself by simply having a sign put on the door. Each of the partners saw the sign and, thinking the other had appointed him, felt it beneath themselves to make enquiries. Selznick continued to operate from the Universal offices without challenge for several months, long enough to see how the business worked. Just as Laemmle had found years before, he saw that he needed a star. Using his 'prestige' as General Manager of Universal he got Clara Kimball Young to agree to move over to his own, not yet formed, Selznick

Pictures. Using Clara Kimball Young's name he rustled up a few investor dollars and so made his first movie. Most of the investors' money was spent on pre-advertising the movie and attracting pre-sales. Selznick was now in the movie business.

His aggressive cult of personality – Lewis J Selznick Presents signs were soon proliferating on Broadway – annoyed his competitors who weren't quite sure where this new rival had sprung from. He further failed to endear himself by stealing their advertising slogans. Mutual were using 'Mutual movies make time fly' which Selznick blatantly adapted to 'Selznick pictures make happy hours'. Famous Players-Lasky used 'Famous players in famous pictures'. Selznick, with untypical modesty, used 'Well known players in well known films'. Selznick made no pretence of originality. He stole anything that wasn't nailed down, like other people's stars: Nazimova, Elsie Janis, Owen Moore (a leading man who was to add to his own lustre by marrying Mary Pickford), both the Talmadge sisters, Norma and Constance. One star he made himself, though he was introduced by Elsie Janis: Olive Thomas. She was to prove his nemesis.

In an incredibly short time Selznick, funded only by monumental gall, had gone from bankrupt to multimillionaire without any apparent effort. That he had also made a bitter enemy out of every other movie Mogul bothered him not at all. Instead Selznick revelled in his new-found wealth. Where other movie men – so recently risen from poverty – tended to cautiously save their money, Selznick spent it lavishly and ostentatiously. He had a twenty-four room apartment, four Rolls Royces, one for every member of the family, each with its own chauffeur. He gave his sons – then aged thirteen and fifteen – thousand-dollar-a-week allowances and kept them well supplied with the sexual services of any of the hundreds of aspiring starlets that flowed through his office in a never-ending stream.

Lewis J had the hottest casting couch in New York. No girl, entering his office, was left in any doubt what would be expected of her should 'His Majesty' give her the sign. Being a star did not excuse you from the sexual summons. Even Nazimova, a convinced lesbian, gritted her teeth and thought of her career, whenever the spirit moved Selznick. It is said that, knowing Nazimova's aversion to men, Selznick took particular delight in summoning her. If even Nazimova had to respond what chance then for the newcomer with no background?

One that came well prepared for Selznick was a doe-eyed, incredibly beautiful sixteen-year-old called Olive Thomas. She came from a depressing mining town in Pennsylvania and an even more depressing background. When she was ten Olive's two sailor brothers developed the idea of supplementing their furlough pay by taking beautiful little Olive along to the local photographer's where she would pose, with her brothers, for the kind of sexually explicit pictures which were known in those days as 'French Postcards'. At twelve she sought adulthood and independence by marrying a miner of twenty-six. On Saturday nights her husband would get drunk and bring his friends home where he would show off Olive and boast of her beautiful body and bedroom skills, often following with a practical demonstration. Olive stood it for two years before she stole the bus fare and ran off to New York. There she came, inevitably, into the social circle of the ubiquitous Elsie Janis, which, equally inevitably, led her to the well worn leather of Ziegfeld's casting couch.

Graduating to Ziegfeld was no problem for Olive who had experienced both public nudity and sex at such an early age. Ziegfeld's costumes, thought scandalous by

most, seemed like overdressing to Olive. Her beauty
ensured that in a very short while she was one of the most
sought-after girls on Broadway. Alberto Vargas, the
leading recorder of feminine beauty, painted her nude at
age fourteen. The contrast between Olive's virginal
appearance and the reality was of piquant interest to
those gift-bearing roués of Broadway. She even found
that her sewer-like language simply added to what passed
for 'charm' to these ageing Romeos.

The lavish attention now being paid to Olive must have
been heady stuff compared to being shown off to a room
full of Saturday night drunks. Curiously those earlier
experiences had developed a taste for rough treatment in
her that her new-found acquaintances couldn't fill. Olive
started seeking out other friends at the seedier end of
Broadway with whom to enjoy a masochistic evening.
This led to many a clash with Ziegfeld's management who
complained that Olive was reporting for work bearing
marks and bruises that not even make-up could entirely
conceal. Olive, repeatedly warned about her conduct,
consulted Elsie Janis. Elsie had the perfect answer for a
girl with a craving for pain. Lewis J Selznick.

Lewis J had grown weary of the simple 'wham-bang'
routine couch encounter. To impress aspirants with his
awesome power he would now leave a girl standing in
front of his desk while he shuffled papers. Without
looking up he would mutter something along the lines of
'I'm not wasting my time talking to girls with clothes
on . . .' The girl could either bolt for the door or stay and
take her cue.

If she stayed Selznick wasn't finished with the humiliation yet. He would produce a riding crop he kept in his
desk drawer and, flicking it menacingly, would launch
into a lecture about the movies having risen to the status

of Art. 'Everyone knows you have to suffer for Art. How much are you ready to suffer?'

The girl, already committed to a state of total or advanced undress, would have to make an instant decision on whether the promise of stardom was worth the more immediate prospect of the crop.

Those that chose to stay and take their chances would find they had merely graduated into compulsory attendance at the Bacchanalian orgies that Selznick threw for buyers and anyone else of influence that might be of help in furthering his meteoric rise. Even star status didn't exempt those under contract from doing their horizontal best for the company.

When Elsie brought the dewy-eyed and incredibly innocent looking Olive into his presence it was with the confidence that they were made for each other. Nevertheless even the hardened Elsie and the lascivious Selznick were somewhat taken aback when Olive entered the room, ignored Selznick and instead studied the huge leather couch for some moments before looking round to speak her first words: 'So that's where I'm going to get fucked, huh?'

Selznick pounced, put her under contract, for various legal reasons, to his seventeen-year-old son Myron, and set Olive off on a career of playing wide-eyed innocent girl-next-door parts. It must have appealed to his by now well developed sense of perversity to see her hailed everywhere as 'The Ideal American Girl' while knowing well her private tastes.

Olive became the star turn at his promotional parties where she found that the rough treatment she craved could be as easily found in a luxurious hotel suite as in a smoky back room downtown.

On-screen men may have lusted after her beautiful body and winsome ways but the Hero, or God, would always intervene at the last moment to save this ideal of virtuous American maidenhood. Soon articles were appearing in Olive's name exhorting her fellow teenagers to respect all that was clean and wholesome in the American Way of Life. Of course Olive didn't have time to write these exhortations herself; she was far too busy orgying! Never for a moment did her adoring audience suspect that their idol lived in a world where alcohol and cocaine were as everyday as corned beef and cabbage was in theirs; where the sexual ebb and flow was no more than a common courtesy.

This carefully constructed image was to be Selznick's undoing for while there was nothing exceptional in Olive Thomas' way of life, the manner of her death was to create an earthquake of revulsion across the entire continent.

Living in the fast lane alongside Olive was a heroin addict, Jack Pickford, brother of that other 'sweet girl next door' Mary Pickford. Jack was, in the public's mind, the male version of sweet Olive. When the couple announced that they were to marry it seemed like the perfect mating. America's sweetheart marries America's 'Ideal Young Man'. They could not have suspected that Jack was tired of waiting in line to enjoy Olive and, in contemplating marriage, was merely trying to promote himself to the front of the queue. Olive, tiring fast of enforced visits to friendly doctors, probably saw the marriage as a convenient cover should anything untoward occur. Certainly neither intended that marriage would affect their life-styles. Their choice of honeymoon destination was Europe, partly because Olive had never been there and partly because America, in an attack of virtue, had introduced Prohibition. Olive was so anxious to get there that she took off without the one essential ingredient for anyone else's honeymoon – a groom. Young Jack was delayed completing a movie, so, naturally, Olive went without him.

Making directly for the Parisian underworld, Olive enjoyed a belated hen party, scoring cocaine, heroin and men in equal parts.

On the morning of 10 September 1922 the floor waiter of the Hotel Crillon in Paris let himself into her suite. He found Olive sprawled naked on the floor clutching a phial of mercury capsules – in those days somewhat venerated as a cure for syphilis, but often fatal.

Years of drugging, drinking, abortions and all night parties had burned young Olive to a cinder. Whether it was suicide – if so for what reason? – or an accidental overdose was never established. Given the rough trade that Olive had hung around with since arriving in Paris it could even have been murder. In the world of drug dealers and pimps a word in the wrong place could prove sufficient motivation.

What is more certain is that it marked the beginning of the end for Lewis J Selznick. The news hit America like an earthquake and the wolf pack, ever lurking for an opportunity, moved in for the kill. Selznick tried to cover up what he could but his rivals' eagerness to feed every last devastating tit-bit to the press ensured that movieland had suffered its first scandal. Lewis J Selznick got the entire blame for corrupting the 'poor child' or, alternatively, for foisting 'that little whore' on to them and their daughters as an example of how young girls should behave. Soon his other stars were jumping ship anxious to avoid having their private lives looked at too closely. Worse, Selznick lost the badly needed confidence of his backers and his bankers. A compulsive gambler, Selznick had often told his sons that there was only one way to treat money and that was to 'spend it, give it away, live beyond your means – it gives a man confidence . . .'

When he lost the money men's confidence there was no reserve with which to fight back. Overnight he went from oriental opulence to penury. There was nowhere Selznick could look to find a friend.

His two sons, having become accustomed to instant gratification of their slightest whim, took it badly. Both took on the mission to avenge themselves on the men who had done their father down. Both, in their own ways, succeeded. Myron built up a hugely powerful agency and delighted in gouging ever greater sums out of the men whom he considered responsible for his father's downfall. David O's revenge was more subtle. He built up a career as an independent producer culminating in making the all-time great *Gone with the Wind* of which much more later.

Throughout the 1910s Hollywood had grown. At the start of the decade Hollywood had a population of 5,000. By 1920 the magnet of the movies had swelled this number to 150,000. The 'industry' had grown along with it. A nickel and dime business in 1910, it now boasted purpose-built picture 'palaces'. Its predominantly working class audience had been joined by a more affluent public and its stories, which had been based upon working class, poverty-line melodramas reflected this. America emerged from the First World War much more aware of a world outside its own frontiers than previously. It was ready to cast off the stern Victorian work and church ethic of pre-war days. The decimation of a whole generation of young men made the girls more competitive and combative than their mothers would have dared to dream of. The daughters had no time for the leisurely courting and betrothal rituals of the pre-war era. They rewrote the book on morality and social behaviour. America was ready for a party to celebrate life and Prohibition did nothing to spoil the mood. If anything the Volstead Act, banning the making or sale of alcohol, only added additional spice. With a youth longing to rebel simply taking a drink was a statement of liberation. Finding and drinking alcohol became a national pursuit.

In keeping with this new spirit the newspapers were also undergoing a revolution in what they considered fit to print. The first tabloid newspaper, *The New York Daily News*, published in 1919, was an instant success. Born out of recognition that the American public had grown more cynical, it started to feed the new appetite for scandal in high places. Hollywood, long grown accustomed to being able to buy its way out of embarrassment, was to suffer from this new aggressive stance.

It was also to provide the media's most productive feeding ground. Never again could Olive Thomas, the 'girl next door', get away with her habitual use of four-letter language in public. Never again would incidents like the following one, which happened in September 1919, go unreported. Olive had been loudly complaining about some injustice she felt she had suffered. She used a stream of four-letter cuss words, delivered at the top of her voice, in the lobby of the Ambassador Hotel. An old lady sitting nearby was so horrified that she dropped her knitting. Olive courteously bent to pick it up for her. As she did so the old lady noticed a magnificent emerald Olive wore on her finger. 'My goodness,' the old lady said, 'how lovely to own such a beautiful thing!' Olive shrugged and smiled. 'It's easy, honey. I got this for two humps with an old Jew in Palm Beach!'

Exit Olive leaving the old lady with mouth agape.

As an allegory, with Olive playing Hollywood, and the old lady, America, it serves well to introduce the twenties.

3

The Twenties – 'You Ain't Heard Nothing Yet'

At the beginning of the twenties the movies had grown from a despised raucous circus side-show to one of the dominant industries in America. Where once the local corn store had been made over for the motion picture show there now stood purpose-built theatres attended, weekly, by 35,000,000 people in the US alone. It was big bucks boom time. More money was being generated, and distributed among the golden inner circle, than even their most profligate members could spend. Onyx bathrooms, tiger-skinned automobiles, extravagant homes and clothes – you could sell a Hollywood success anything.

None were more successful than those street-wise enough to have got into movies before anyone knew what they were going to become. These same men, young then, were to dominate Hollywood for the next four decades. They were known as the Hollywood Moguls. Our image of them is that of pot-bellied, loud-mouthed cigar-smoking, middle-aged cretins. None of them was stupid, most were under-educated and English was not the most common mother tongue but then, in the twenties, they were all surprisingly young. In 1920 Louis B Mayer was the 'old man' of Hollywood. He was thirty-five. His legendary right-hand man, Irving Thalberg, was twenty-one. Jack Warner was twenty-eight, B P Schulberg, later head of Paramount, then of Famous Players-Lasky, was also twenty-eight. Harry Cohn, already scraping the barrel on Poverty Row, destined to become the much-hated head of Columbia, was twenty-nine. Darryl F Zanuck, already in town working his way through the

Sennett Bathing Beauties was, in 1920, just eighteen years old. At fifteen he had joined the army and fought in the trenches of France; here was a young man in a hurry. He didn't have to hurry long – at twenty-seven, in 1929, he became head of production at Warner's.

The war years had been kind to Hollywood. Prior to the First World War Europe, especially Germany, had led the way from crudity to creativity, but the war years had wreaked havoc. Hollywood, safely out of the reach of bombs or shells, had filled the vacuum. As the twenties began it dominated the world's screens as it does to this day.

If Hollywood had changed so had America. Small-town men had travelled abroad, encountered new ideas and seen death and bloodshed. No more were they willing to accept hand-me-down sermons on the evils of this or that. They had met evil face to face and knew the stench of it. Women's attitudes changed too. Skirts started reaching for the sky. Corsets were out, so newer slim-line figures were in. There was no point in simpering in the shadows like Mary Pickford, Blanche Sweet and the other 'good girl' heroines. If you wanted a man you had to get out there and fight for one – no holds barred! Nowhere was this change reflected faster than on the movie screen, which further fostered the trend. Prohibition had made drinking a symbol of this rejection of old values. A new phenomenon appeared – the flapper which, curiously, was the death of the old-style 'vamp'. No longer was it necessary to be born in the shadow of the pyramids to want pre-marital sex – the girl next door was doing it. She also started talking about 'it', reading about 'it' and, very soon, she was doing 'it' on the movie screen.

Hollywood needed a new kind of woman.

Louise Brooks not only epitomized this post-war

woman but also was the archetypal Hollywood 'discovery'. At fifteen she had been an under-dressed chorine in that crucible of screen talent – the Ziegfeld Follies. Equally predictably she was pursued by the many young and old stage door Johnnies. Almost as soon as she had cast her first layer of clothing she was set up, at fifteen, by millionaire John Lock. So accepted was the inevitability of rich men having girl-child mistresses from the Follies that Louise was lodged at the swankiest address in town, The Marguery. Not bad at fifteen.

Unfortunately John Lock had business to take care of other than the winsome Miss Brooks and he was soon getting restive at the amount of unauthorized traffic passing through his luxury love nest. Matters came to a decided head when, acting on information received, he, one night, let himself into the apartment to find his adolescent mistress passionately returning the naked embraces of a screenwriter called Townsend Martin. It wasn't so much what they were doing that upset Lock, so much as that they kept right on doing it even after they had registered his presence. Refusing Louise's invitation to join them, John instead – unfashionably – stormed out of the apartment. Before Louise had finished in the bathroom she found she had lost her meal ticket, the apartment and her job. Ziegfeld had strict rules about almost nothing except being caught. One piece of luck remained to her. Her erstwhile lover, Townsend, suggested she might try her luck out at the Long Island studios of a company called Famous Players-Lasky where Townsend could introduce her.

The introduction was to Walter Wanger, then head of production. Having been schooled by Ziegfeld and coached by Townsend, Louise knew exactly what to expect. Wanger was only half way through asking her, 'What makes you think you have what it takes to be a movie actress?' when Louise responded by taking off her clothes, reclining elegantly on the essential couch and enquiring: 'How's this for starters?'

Immediately realizing Louise's potential, Wanger placed her under contract that same afternoon. When Famous Players-Lasky moved west to California, Louise went with them. There she was to make nine more movies. None of them had much impact but her glowing beauty, which still shines through today, and the spirit in which she approached her work, ensured the steady renewal of her contracts. Louise didn't much care. Movies were only an adjunct to her real interests – night clubs and millionaires. Her all-night partying made problems for directors trying to coax a performance from the sleep-deprived teenager and, finally, those problems piled up into a mountain until she found herself 'let go'. Louise went to Europe where she was to make the only two memorable movies of her career: *Pandora's Box* and *Diary of a Lost Girl* (the latter might have been her biography), both for German genius Georg W Pabst. Pabst nursed an almost unrequited passion for Louise throughout their association but was equipped with neither the energy nor the money to make the pace set by Louise and her coterie of millionaire admirers. They considered that crossing the Atlantic in pursuit of a fervent night with Louise well worth the price of the ticket.

After the completion of *Pandora's Box* Pabst tried to free himself from Louise and stay away. Louise hardly noticed until the night she found her supply of ardent millionaires was running low. Unnoticed by her, Wall Street had crashed and with it the fortunes of many of her erstwhile dinner companions. Re-engaging her mind to making movies she discovered that dear old unrequited Pabst was planning a new movie without her. Well aware of Pabst's passion for her, she summoned him to her Paris hotel suite. There she told him that she wanted to make *Diary of a Lost Girl* with him, and, yes, the bedroom was this way.

Their affair lasted only the length of the shooting schedule, at the end of which Louise found that Pabst's devotion was somewhat lessened. Louise returned to Hollywood expecting acclamation for her two European triumphs only to find that success in 'art' movies meant little in the fun factory – especially since sound had replaced silence.

Louise made some extremely boring pictures with downmarket Republic and then drifted to New York and into a more direct sex-for-sale lifestyle. These years are covered in merciful obscurity until she was to re-emerge as a film historian and writer of note.

Louise Brooks was not only too beautiful but also too intelligent to take seriously the Hollywood whirlwind. She would have made the perfect F Scott Fitzgerald heroine. She certainly lived the twenties' image to the hilt, but she wasn't alone in that.

Right on the heels of the Olive Thomas suicide scandal came an even bigger scandal. Ex-plumber's mate Fatty Arbuckle had been taken on at the Sennett Studio as a $3-dollar-a-day extra in 1913. By 1917 he was at Paramount and being paid $5,000 a week! In 1921 America's favourite fat-boy funny man renewed his contract at Paramount for no less than $1 million a year! The overweight comedian had plenty to celebrate and when Fatty celebrated Hollywood held its breath. 'Party' was synonymous with 'orgy' in Fatty's vocabulary so few of the stars, starlets and extras who received invitations could have had any illusions as to the expected order of events. To accept an invitation from Arbuckle was tantamount to acquiescence. Half Hollywood was only too happy to accept Fatty's invitation to share his good fortune with a long weekend of booze and girls at San Francisco's plush Hotel St Francis where a whole floor had been reserved for the festivities. The lure for the girls was the certainty that they would have a chance to meet, to say the least, some of the most luminous names in Hollywood, and who knew where that might lead?

The party was due to start on Saturday, run through Sunday and over the convenient holiday provided by the Labour Day weekend. No one was expecting polite conversation and cucumber sandwiches, which makes later testimony even harder to understand. Carloads of girls and hangers-on headed north from Hollywood jostling on the highway with trucks bringing in the ocean of bootleg booze ordered for the festivities. The party lasted three days. Among the many starlets was one Virginia Rappe. She had been around the fringes of Hollywood for some time, been through the Sennett school for young hopefuls, and had a few useful roles in smaller features. She was on the brink of bigger things when she went up to help out the girls at the St Francis. She went there mainly on the advice of one Maude Delmont who had pointed out that Virginia was an ageing twenty-five and needed 'all the help she could get' from someone as powerful as Arbuckle. At some point on Monday – it was Labour Day and so no one had work to go to – Virginia finally caught the eye of Fatty who took her by the hand into a bedroom and, somewhat anti-socially, considering the prevailing mood, locked the door. Ten minutes later the other guests stirred from their drunken revels to realize that cries of an unusual and disturbing nature were coming from the bedroom. Nobody intervened since it was considered likely Fatty was giving Virginia a good, if unusual, time. No one took notice until Fatty emerged from the bedroom and told some of the girls to get Virginia dressed and 'out of here'. They went into the bedroom and found Virginia moaning in pain. They took her to hospital where she was found to have internal haemorrhaging. Five days later she died, and the rumour mill went into overtime. Fatty was accused of everything from damaging the girl with a champagne bottle to having had several helpers hold her down while he jammed a huge piece of ice into her vagina. Maude Delmont testified at Fatty's *three* trials that when she had gone into the bedroom intending to dress Virginia she couldn't do so because her clothing was reduced to rags – strange testimony since, according to another guest at the party, Virginia had been wearing precisely nothing when she went into the bedroom. Maybe she had been a 'victim' of the Sunday night party game when volunteer girls lined up to have their clothes ripped from them by Fatty on the promise of even better ones being provided from a nearby exclusive store. That store being closed for Labour Day could have accounted for Virginia's naked presence on the Monday.

With everyone's favourite sexual fantasy being trotted out and attributed to Arbuckle it came as something of an anti-climax when, through three trials, two juries failed to convict and were dismissed, and the third unanimously acquitted him, adding a rider to air their opinion that 'a grave injustice' had been done Fatty and they could find no evidence whatsoever of him having committed a crime.

Fatty was free but was to remain condemned. The American public were not prepared to accept that the funny man they'd made so rich hadn't been guilty of 'something'. Fatty's main guilt was in being found out. Adolph Zukor, his Paramount boss, had good reason to be glad he'd left the St Francis late on Sunday. Four years earlier he'd been less lucky when attending an Arbuckle celebratory orgy and had been caught by police with his trousers down. That particular party had been to celebrate

Fatty's first contract with Paramount. A passer-by had looked through a hotel window and seen a naked Fatty leading a conga-line of ten equally naked girls with Zukor and other Paramount executives cheering them on. Zukor had, on that occasion, managed to divert scandal by buying off the cops, the District Attorney and everybody else that got wind of it. Zukor had, prior to Fatty's first trial, tried similar tactics in San Francisco but without success. Now, not being personally involved, he pre-judged the outcome of the trial and cancelled the very contract that Arbuckle had gone to San Francisco to celebrate. The debacle must rank as one of the most expensive parties in history since it cost Arbuckle his contract, his houses, and his cars along with his entire career.

This sudden and crushing end to an 'unstoppable' career, you might be forgiven for thinking, would give pause to other orgifiers in the Hollywood firmament. Not so. That same year Alla Nazimova, a lady once described by Darryl F Zanuck as 'Queen of the Movie Whores', threw one for the opening of her hotel/guest bungalow complex which she called The Garden of Allah. Everyone was told to come in Oriental costume which, for the men, meant dressing as Arab princes and for the women the minimum that decency permitted. Nazimova herself appeared in the costume of Salome, a part she had recently played on screen, and left little to the heightened imagination. Betty Blythe went one better and wore her costume from her recent role as the Queen of Sheba, which consisted of a row of beads over her bare breasts. Rising young actor Rudolph Valentino wore much the same as Betty. A whole galaxy of stars were in attendance trying to outdo each other in matters undress; Norma and Constance Talmadge, Clara Kimball Young, and the girl she was to share scandal with, eighteen-year-old Mary

Miles Minter, on screen a rival to Mary Pickford. Mary was out of the same mould as Olive Thomas, and this night was anxious to show her own true self. Alice Terry, Dorothy Gish, Pearl White, Lya de Putti, Colleen Moore and many others turned out in Oriental undress for the festivities. Only Mary Pickford spoiled the fun by coming as Little Lord Fauntleroy! Outdoing this outrageous bunch of movie queens took some doing, but one Barbara LaMarr, known after her early death as 'The Girl Who Was Too Beautiful', managed it. She took a bungalow by the poolside and hung out a boardwalk-type sign reading: 'Come One Come All'. Nazimova, it was generally anticipated was going to provide the climax to the first evening – the party lasted two days – by repeating her highly erotic dance of the seven veils, which had recently shocked America, but this time removing the seventh veil. Someone's timing was off because, just as her music was cued, the whole proceedings were interrupted by the arrival of some sixteen or twenty naked starlets who, whooping with joy, leapt straight into the swimming pool where they were shortly joined by many smiling men trying out for the Olympics. Nazimova retired to her own bungalow where she received many of her women admirers in mutual consolation.

Nazimova was the centre of Hollywood's social circle at the time. Being in her forties and still a star was no mean achievement. Her role as mentor to many of the girls in Hollywood came naturally to her and she soon expanded her interest to take in the homosexual male stars, running a kind of protective marriage bureau when their sexual tastes threatened to go public. Two direct beneficiaries of this were Rudolph Valentino and Ramon Navarro. When rumours of the Great Lover's personal preference for boys started to circulate Nazimova arranged for him to marry one of her 'protégées', Jean Aker. The marriage was one for the record only and nobody felt moved to change their sleeping arrangements. The marriage was not, however, destined to last long. Miss Aker tired of the many jokes about the marriage circulating in Hollywood and, to the astonishment of the entire female population of the United States, divorced Valentino. Nazimova, undaunted, produced another bride from among her many girl friends – one Winifred Hudnutt. Now it was obvious that nobody named Winifred Hudnutt could marry Valentino, so Nazimova had her rechristened Natascha Rambova. Nazimova must have been temporarily out of stock when Ramon Navarro, Valentino's screen rival, but off-screen good friend, ran into similar difficulties, since she married him herself.

To the public the true embodiment of the twenties was Clara Bow. Clara had suffered chronic insomnia since the time her mother crept into her bedroom with a knife and threatened to kill her for having sent in her picture to a magazine promotional contest, first prize for which was a small role in a movie! Mother was prevented from saving Clara from becoming 'one of those whores strutting in front of the movie cameras for the pleasure of men' Clara won that contest and so began her career with the promised walk-on in *Beyond The Rainbow*. Not coming from a show business background, and having no friends in the business, the wide-eyed seventeen-year-old hadn't been told what every other aspirant already knew. Terrified at what retribution her neurotic mother might wreak if she succumbed, Clara refused all offers of the 'couch'. Her part in *Beyond The Rainbow* was left on the cutting room floor, but the magazine that had promoted the contest, *Motion Picture Classic*, had played up the story of 'their' protégée, complete with photographs. These were seen by an impecunious but talent-hungry director named Elmer Clifton. He put her into a picture, *Down to the Sea in Ships*, masquerading as a boy. She was noticed by another impecunious producer, B P Schulberg. His speciality was finding raw young talent and training it up in his Preferred Pictures, so as to loan it out to other studios at a big profit to himself. He saw a likely vehicle in Clara. He signed her for $50 a week and promised that she would never again have to sleep alone. Clara had found, during the making of *Down to the Sea in Ships*, that Elmer Clifton had the sovereign remedy for her insomnia – sexual exhaustion. It was an appetite that Clara was never to lose.

B P Schulberg had yet another sovereign remedy – work. He put Clara into a punishing schedule of fourteen movies in the first year of her contract. With such a shotgun approach Clara couldn't fail to make some kind of impact on moviegoers. Only a minority of these pictures – fortunately for Clara – were made by Schulberg's own company, Preferred. Most were loan-outs and the Schulberg family fortunes flourished on the back of them. When Paramount showed interest in her, Schulberg's price for Clara's contract was that he go along with her. The pictures got better and the parts bigger until she hit the big time with *Mantrap* in 1926. She was now so popular that she was used as 'insurance' when Paramount introduced newcomer Eddie Cantor in his first film. When Clara starred in the movie version of the Elinor Glyn book *It*, she triumphantly consolidated her status, and ever afterwards became known as the *It* girl. By 1929 she was named in several fan polls as the most popular actress, but she had never made the fabulous sums her contemporaries did. At the height of her fame she had just about risen to a respectable $3,000 a week and was to briefly touch $5,000 before her riveting sex life caused her downfall.

Clara's patent insomnia cure led to difficulties in her

emotional life. With a whole string of lovers, men like Gilbert Roland, Gary Cooper – whose reputation was that of a horse – Bela Lugosi, and director Victor Fleming, any girl might have felt she was well served. Not Clara. Victor Fleming once did all he could for her but after leaving her bedroom hung around the house only to see Clara leave. Victor followed to see her cruise the boulevards picking up men, taking them to a motel and then going in search of another! Gas station attendants were not safe from her. Floor crew in the studios felt threatened, until one Saturday afternoon Clara found the ideal for which she had been searching – football teams! That particular afternoon the team was the USC's 'Thundering Herd', The Trojans – also the name of a popular male sheath. Clara eyed the mountain of male meat and came to their changing room with a unique offer. Every time the team won they were invited up to her house for a celebration.

Expecting lots of gorgeous starlets the team were initially disappointed to find only Clara and one other girl waiting to entertain them. Clara soon dispelled their blues by telling them that she had read a story about the wife of a Roman emperor who had, in one night, opened up to half of the male Roman population. Surely *they* could come to some arrangement? They did and the Trojans' winning ratio rose. At first the team coach was delighted with the extra incentive the 'boys' were getting up at Clara's Georgian house in Beverly Hills, but later he became alarmed at the signs of decline in the team's performance. Clara, on the other hand, was making no complaints. Her source of night time solace dried up when the coach imposed a ban on visits to Clara's, even going so far as to post a notice to this effect in the team's changing room. Among the dedicated sportsmen on the Trojan team was a rangy running back called John

Wayne. Clara rewarded him with a scene shifter's job at the studios, where he provided much between-takes entertainment, until he realized he was once more playing on a team!

Throughout these years of plenty Clara had made strenuous efforts to set her father up in one business after another. Each had failed and cost her a barrel-load of money. As chaotic in all things as she was in her emotional life, it was B P Schulberg, now more a father figure than a lover, who advised her to hire a disciplined girl secretary to straighten herself out. Clara did. Unfortunately the girl promptly fell in love with Clara's father and married him. Now Clara was stuck with both of them to support and still no secretary. Her next choice was even more disastrous – a girl called Daisy Devoe. Daisy had been working as a hairdresser at the studio when, one night, Clara invited her back to her house to make up the numbers in a poker game. Daisy knew, going in, how Clara's poker sessions usually ended, but was curious to see for herself. She saw even greater chances when she woke next morning to find herself in bed with Clara and Gary Cooper. It was heady stuff for a working girl. Daisy made herself Clara's confidante and within days was her live-in companion and clothes holder when the action switched to the bedroom.

Talking pictures were threatening and every silent star – no matter how big – saw their asylum vanishing. Daisy got Clara a voice coach and together they worked day and night on saving Clara's career.

One morning, over breakfast, Clara found herself forced to ask passing lover and cowboy star Rex Bell for a loan. Bell was astonished. He knew that Clara was making far more money than he was, and immediately suspected something was wrong in the Bow household. He went to Clara's attorney and had him obtain a court order for the opening of Daisy's bank deposit vault. Inside were found many of the choicest items of Clara's jewellery, fur coats and hundreds of cancelled cheques all made out in favour of Daisy. In the three years Daisy had been managing Clara's affairs she had managed to divert huge sums to her own account. When the law threatened, Daisy played what she fondly believed was her ace defence. She had a bundle of letters written to Clara from some of Hollywood's biggest names, and a whole bundle of Clara's – unposted – replies. Within this collected correspondence were many explicit suggestions about what the writers would like to do, or have done to them, on their next meeting. Additionally, Daisy smugly informed the lawyers, she had a complete list of the participants in Clara's orgies. Clara's lawyers tried to call her bluff, but undaunted, Daisy went over their heads to Clara's studio, Paramount. Paramount had a problem. The sound revolution was making huge inroads into their stock of stars, and contracts were being lapsed wholesale as the studio took the opportunity to drop their expensive but now damaged silent stars. Daisy's demand for $125,000 for the letters and diaries was not seriously considered. Instead the studio called the cops and accused Daisy of attempted extortion. Clara, when told of this, had a nervous breakdown. There was nothing she or her lawyers could do to intervene and stop the legal process begun by Paramount. Instead she was forced to attend court where the pressing crowds had a chance to look into the tearful, bloated face of the girl that had shaped thousands of lives as she listened to the most intimate details of her sex life and personal preferences read in open court.

Daisy did her revengeful best to complete the demolition of Clara. She told the gaping millions that Clara gave her the money and jewellery as gifts but 'has probably forgotten since she was often too drunk to write her own cheques or even to remember which man she'd just spent the night with'. It was from Daisy's evidence that we know about the Thundering Herd and Clara's unique reward system.

The trial degenerated into a circus with both sides giving tear-choked press conferences full of accusations and counter-charges combined with, from Clara, contrite confessions.

Clara, who had never wanted the prosecution in the first place, was backpedalling hard. Hearing from her attorney that the judge was ready to convict on all eighteen counts, Clara took the astonishing step of personally pleading with him for leniency. The judge gave weight to Clara's plea and, convicted on one count only, sending Daisy to jail for eighteen months. The reason for Clara's action only became clear later. Clara knew that Daisy had told less than half of what she knew. Clara was trying to protect her friends by pleading for mercy.

Those 'friends' repaid Clara by turning their collective backs on her. Her weight ballooning, her career wallowing and soon to be sunk without trace, she married the man who had started it all – Rex Bell. Together they fled Hollywood for the quieter reaches of Nevada where, at the ripe old age of twenty-six, she went into hiding.

Clara had lost everything but hope. Every year she would send a pathetic postcard to columnist Hedda Hopper with a one-line message: 'Do you remember me?' Nobody did.

Clara had lived through seventeen years of grinding poverty, ten years of incandescent stardom and thirty years as a has-been before, after innumerable breakdowns, she died alone and penniless at age sixty. Maybe, sometime during those last thirty years, she might have considered that her mother knew best after all.

If Clara was insatiable she had her male counterpart in

Sydney Chaplin – Charlie's brother. Sydney had, briefly, been the better known of the two, but now Charlie had outstripped him in every way except one: girls. Charlie liked them young but Sydney liked them often. His astonished Boswell, the youthful Darryl F Zanuck, reported that Sydney would consider a day in which he made love to four girls as average. Having started out laying waste Sennett's Bathing Beauties, Sydney extended his activities to anything under twenty and wearing a skirt. His pride in his skills was not something he kept hidden Zanuck once challenged him to make good his boast that he could pick up any of the teenage girls coming out of Hollywood High School. Zanuck drove him there, pointed out the target and watched as Sydney went over and started talking to the girl. Within minutes he was handing the flushed-faced girl into the open tourer and asking Zanuck to drive them somewhere 'peaceful'. Zanuck did and then sat red-faced, and facing front, while Sydney made good his boast on the back seat. Sydney was not one to rest on his laurels. He asked Zanuck to come up with a really hard one next time!

Zanuck thought he had found the perfect opportunity when he and Sydney were booked into the Coronada Hotel for the weekend. The Coronada was popular with honeymooners at the time. Zanuck pointed out an embarrassed bride booking in with her brand-new husband. '*That* is impossible!' he told Sydney. Zanuck lost sight of Sydney during lunch and spent an hour looking around the grounds of the hotel in an attempt to find him. Returning to the main building Zanuck found himself being paged. He learned that Sydney wanted him to come to his room immediately. On entering Darryl was confronted with the sight of a naked Sydney enjoying the oral administrations of an equally naked, no longer blushing, bride! It was that incident that left Zanuck in lifetime awe of his friend's prowess and a lifetime need to emulate it. What Zanuck probably never knew was that the Coronada incident was a carefully staged set-up. The 'bride' was an extra named Elizabeth McNeill and the groom was also hired from Central Casting; his name is lost to history. Sydney had 'pushed' Zanuck's choice with the skill of a card sharp. Nevertheless Sydney's notoriety as a girl chaser was legendary around Hollywood – a place not easily impressed – and his many exploits genuinely astonishing. 'Hollywood,' he once said, 'is a town full of pretty girls dying to get into bed. You'd have to be an idiot not to take advantage.'

But what of brother Charlie? Surely after his salutary lesson over the business of bunnikin Mildred Harris he changed his ways? If you believe that, you forget his long-nurtured lust for 'the sweetest little thing you ever saw' – Lita Grey. Lita had been a winsome six-year-old when Mildred was getting hers. Now, after nine years – and how they must have dragged by for Chaplin! – of training he finally judged Lita ready for 'the big one'. This may sound like a deep-laid sinister plot on Charlie's part but he was walking headlong into a trap, developed over many years, by Lita's mother, Nana McMurray. Nana was the epitome of the pushing Hollywood mother. Since she had played a small part in the drama over Mildred Harris, some ten years before, she couldn't have been unaware of where her plans for little Lita were going to lead. Lita herself was no more than a wide-eyed pawn in the whole game. Charlie must have been the blindest man in existence not to have seen the trap.

It was Charlie's habit to shoot his masterly little comedies at snail's pace. His longer pictures were often in production over a year, each fragment carefully constructed, gone over and, often, reshot. It was his studio and he was worth in excess of $20 million so he could afford his freedom. When the Muse failed he would retire to his office to brood. Often he would take by the hand some pretty extra girl to assist in his deeper thinking.

Little Lita became his co-consulter of the Muse some-time in 1923 when, according to Lita, he was seized with a sudden fit of passion during the filming of the dance hall scene in *The Gold Rush*. He rushed little Lita off to his office where 'his body writhed furiously against mine and frightened me'. Delighted with this development her mother calmed Lita's fears, explained what all this 'furious writhing' was about and sent her little girl back into the fray. A startled Lita gave up her virginity during a naked romp at Charlie's house one night while Charlie boasted he could have any one of a thousand girls but 'wanted to be with naughty you'. In early November 1924 the inevitable result was that Nana was able, trium-phantly, to confront Charlie with the news that little Lita was pregnant. Charlie was astounded. Through many thousands of couplings he had never made anyone preg-nant before and had convinced himself he was incapable of it. Medical confirmation was obtained, combined with the appearance of Nana's brother, a lawyer conveniently enough, to point out the law, to a man who already knew to his cost that sex with an underage girl was illegal. Getting her pregnant, ruminated Charlie, was going to be expensive. Charlie reacted as any decent red-blooded male would. He did the decent thing and offered her first the money to have an abortion and secondly $20,000 to marry somebody else! But her Uncle Ed was on hand to threaten a paternity suit and a statutory rape charge and managed to moderate Charlie's thinking. He took Lita south to Sonora for what he hoped would be a quiet wedding. On the way he romantically suggested she should throw herself from the train, but nothing he could say could dissuade Lita from using her return ticket in the name of Mrs Charles Chaplin.

The wedding was anything but quiet. The press turned out in bus loads. The world had changed since Charlie had taken dewy-eyed Miss Mildred Harris south. Then Charlie had been twenty-six, just ten years older than his 'pregnant' bride. People pursed their lips but since there was only a ten-year gap and Charlie was such a lovable clown, what could anyone expect? The world had grown more cynical since. The bride's age was the same but Charlie was now thirty-six and 'should have known better'. Had America known that little Lita was already pregnant the resulting outcry could have driven Charlie out of the movie business. It wasn't until seven months later, on 28 June 1925, that those who could count worked it all out. Charlie had been telling friends how he 'couldn't stand' his bride, but must have overcome his repugnance at least once more since, almost exactly nine months after the birth of Charles Chaplin Jnr, another son, Sydney, made his appearance.

During the months of his marriage the McMurrays moved in on Charlie, determined to make his life a living hell. All night boozy parties – Charlie had never been known to throw even a tea party previously, although he loved those that other people paid for – became the order of the day. Mother Nana was in residence claiming that her daughter was 'too young and inexperienced' to properly run a household. Finally Charlie could stand it no longer and fled to New York.

This was what Nana had been waiting for. Uncle Ed got an order sequestering Charlie's assets on behalf of Lita, who filed for divorce. Charlie, aware of the kind of settlement an eighteen-year-old mother of his two sons could get, issued a statement that he still loved his wife and wanted to stay married. Uncle Ed countered by publishing a fifty-page statement, on sale at twenty-five cents a copy, which gave full details of the intimate exchanges in the marital bedroom. These juicy titbits were culled from a journal kept by the doting Nana as, daily, Lita reported on the previous night's events as any daughter would. The journal revealed that Chaplin had had no fewer than 'five long-term mistresses' during his twenty-five-month marriage; had often suggested livening up the marriage bed by the introduction of another young girl; had insisted on 'unnatural' practices; had threatened to kill her and said he wanted nothing more than to have sex with her in front of a camera and/or an audience. This last statement led to a rash of 'stag reels' being produced with Chaplin lookalikes which are nowhere near as funny as Charlie himself would undoubtedly have been. Chaplin ignored the wave of raucous laughter that rolled across the country from one bar-room to another. In fact the issue of the journal revealed to the public the vicious nature of the campaign the McMurrays were mounting. Public opinion started moving Charlie's way. The McMurrays, however, had one last card to play. They hinted that the 'five mistresses' were all well known movie stars and their names, withheld until now, would shortly be revealed. Charlie caved in, since one of those names was dynamite that could have blasted both his professional career and social life to untraceable fragments. He settled for close to a million dollars and the McMurrays went out of his life to get on with celebrating a job well done. It had taken close to twelve years, but the waiting had been worth it.

The one name that was worth more than a million dollars to Charlie was that of Marion Davies. Marion had many times consoled the stricken Chaplin when he had fled the living hell the McMurrays had made of his home. The most notorious occasion was just a week before his enforced marriage. Hearst had issued an invitation to

Hollywood's inner clique to be on board his luxury yacht, *Oneida*, for a short weekend cruise. Marion was to be hostess to a group of wives, mistresses and assorted business partners. Among them were an obscure journalist, Louella Parsons, Chaplin and a producer, Thomas Ince. Ince was at that time credited with being one of the few true gentlemen in the movie industry. The party was being given to celebrate his forty-third birthday and to discuss the possibility of Cosmopolitan (Hearst's own production company) setting up shop in Ince's studios.

Champagne flowed freely and twenty-seven-year-old Marion began to feel that her gay mood was not going to be satisfied by sixty-three-year-old William. Instead she slipped off for some pre-bedtime dalliance with another guest. Hearst, ever alert, noticed her missing and went looking for her. He found her, dress hiked, in an undignified position under a heaving male. Not stopping to identify the man, Hearst threatened to kill him, only to realize he had left his revolver in his cabin. When he left to retrieve it, Marion started screaming for help while her lover slipped away. Ince, hearing the frightened screams, went into the bedroom where Hearst discovered him trying to quieten the hysterical Marion. Jumping to the conclusion that Ince was the heaving man of a few minutes ago, Hearst fired a fatal shot into Ince's temple. A hush descended over the assembled guests and thoughts turned to what was to be done. No one suggesting confessing to the truth, they all agreed that Ince had never been on board and was, in fact, due to die of acute indigestion in a car hurrying him home to his loved ones in Hollywood from San Diego.

The San Diego coroner was happy to confirm this diagnosis, and also richer – the hole in the man's head was an obvious irrelevance. Within days Ince had been cremated, so ending all further investigation, Ince's widow had been set up with a trust fund by Hearst,

Louella Parsons got a plum lifetime's job with the Hearst press – she chose to stay in Hollywood and become a show biz columnist – and Charles Chaplin left town to marry little Lita. Well he might, because Louella's new career and the curious case of the 'heaving man' were not unconnected. Louella had seen him leaving Marion's cabin and had also seen Ince go in after Hearst went to look for his gun. What Louella knew was that the wrong man had got shot. The heaving man was none other than Charlie himself. Such a close call must have made him consider that marrying Lita wasn't such a bad deal after all. Maybe all his troubles would have been over if he had invited Hearst to the reception! Instead he survived to create even more scandals, one a decade, in fact, so we shall have to return to him in later chapters.

Meanwhile, back in the unreal world of landlubbing Hollywood, the girls were still pouring in. Treading the well worn path from Ziegfeld's Follies to Mack Sennett's couch was a girl who was there the night they opened the Garden of Allah – Barbara LaMarr. She was a sixteen-year-old veteran when she first came to Hollywood and was dubbed 'The Girl Who Was Too Beautiful'. Beautiful she was, and soon much in demand. Barbara was at all the best parties and, like Clara Bow, enjoyed them all. In ten years she had six husbands and a couple of thousand lovers. She boasted that she liked lovers like bunches of roses, 'by the dozen', and that her idea of a good night's sleep was to snooze between bouts of love-making. Somehow she managed to fit in more than twenty unmemorable movies in those ten years. Just as well, since those years were all she had coming. She died, aged twenty-six, of 'natural causes', drugged, burned out and exhausted. Her only really memorable bequest to Hollywood was to have her name reused when a certain Hedy Kiesler came to

town in the thirties and was rechristened Lamarr in
memory of Barbara.

Adolph Zukor, prime mover in Paramount's fortunes,
could consider that he had had more than his fair share of
ill-luck. Having started the decade by losing Fatty Arbuckle to scandal, he was about to be hit by a series of
scandals that, virtually, wiped out his top talent. His
senior director was a man called William Desmond
Taylor. During the night of 1 February 1922 someone
murdered him. That was bad enough, but worse was
discovered when the Paramount clean-up squad got to
Taylor's house. Everyone knew that Taylor was a dedicated womanizer; what they didn't know was that he was
also a collector of his conquests' underwear – all carefully
annotated as to owner and date of surrender – a collector
of photographs, some signed on the back by the lady
posing indecently on the front, and love letters from half
of Hollywood's leading ladies – among them Edna Purviance, Mabel Normand and Zukor's young and supposedly
innocent star, Mary Miles Minter. Even more embarrassing was the discovery of similarly explicit letters from
Mary's mother, Charlotte Selby. It seems that Charlotte
had been romancing William Desmond Taylor, believing
that by doing so she was furthering her daughter's
chances, without realizing that little Mary Miles was also
delivering on her own account! The murderer was never
found. A strange figure dressed as a man but 'walking like
a woman' was seen leaving the house that night. Rumour
had it that Mary's mother, on discovering William Desmond Taylor's cynical duplicity, had taken revenge. It
was known that she owned a similar calibre gun to the
murder weapon and had recently been taking shooting
lessons. Whatever the truth, now never to be known,
Zukor had lost his top director and, as events were to
prove, Mary Miles Minter's career was over. Mabel

Normand's pictures were boycotted and she slipped gracefully into forced retirement.

Zukor might have hoped for some respite, but with the rumblings of William Desmond Taylor's death still reverberating, Paramount was to be hit again. This time it was their top male star, Wallace Reid. There had been hushed-up rumours of drug dependency in the Taylor/Minter scandal, but they couldn't be hidden when Wallace Reid, Paramount's all-American boy was taken away to a lunatic asylum where he died, in a padded cell, in January 1923. His wife, Florence, started out on a nation-wide lecture tour to warn about the evils of alcohol and drugs, laying the blame on Wallace's friends and associates. Out of deference to Zukor and the other Hollywood Tsars she failed to mention that the studios themselves had often been the first suppliers of cocaine, which they regularly used to fuel their stars through their punishing work schedules. Barbara LaMarr lived her short life on a heady cocktail of almost anything that came to hand. Another victim was Alma Rubens, who burned out during this decade. Juanita Hansen, another veteran of the Sennett school, ended her career in a blaze of drug-connected headlines. Hollywood, hit by scandal after scandal, felt it was time to do something. The 'something' they did was bring in William Hays, supposedly Mr Clean, to rule over them and take care of the moral side of things. Hays' job, in reality was to serve as figurehead, a mask behind which the money mill could keep grinding. Hays brought out his notorious list of 'do's and dont's' for the movie industry which were universally ignored until the thirties. Hollywood's founding fathers paid him $100,000 a year to stay out of their way. Hollywood continued swinging its way through the twenties until overtaken by two events which rocked it to its foundations – the coming of sound and, in the following year, the Wall Street Crash.

Sound ended the careers of many of the lustrous twenties' stars, and the Wall Street Crash wiped out whatever savings they had made.

Where the twenties had been born out of war and a shortage of eligible men, and bred the resolve to have a good time, the thirties began with genuine deprivation, unemployment and misery.

There were many casualties but some survived. One of the least likely survivors was a girl who had barely got started when the talkies arrived. She had played a series of flappers and good-time girls in small pictures but had made little impact. She seemed ripe for the chop. In fact she triumphed over it all and became one of the most enduring of all of them. Her name was Joan Crawford.

4
Joan Crawford – A Star is Porn

In her later years as reigning Queen of Hollywood Joan was much given to making condemnatory statements about the falling moral values in Hollywood.

'When I see some of the things that young actresses are prepared to do on the screen these days, I just thank God that nothing like that happened in my day. Nudity and explicit sexual acts, as shown on screen these days, are shocking and embarrassing. I would never have agreed to do half the things I see on screen today.' Joan was speaking with all the zeal of the reformed.

Joan was born on the wrong side of the tracks in San Antonio, Texas, as Billie Cassin. Her father deserted the family, and Mother moved both little Billy and herself to Kansas City. Mother did the thing she knew best – home entertaining – so little Billy was sent out each day to find her own salvation. Lacking any formal education she learned to beg or scrub floors at the age of eight. She was picked up for not attending school and her mother solved both her personal problem and Billy's by hiring her out to a succession of boarding schools where Billy paid her tuition by doing the cleaning. She was, reportedly, constantly beaten for inefficient work, and life must have been a misery for the confused and deprived little girl.

At twelve something magical happened. The street waif turned, overnight it seemed to her distracted mother, into a bosomy young lady who got wolf whistles in the street. Mother took her daughter back and gave her a run-down on the family business.

Thereafter the apartment mother and daughter shared

was often besieged by men driving expensive cars, and mother and daughter were both doing well.

Joan was popular with the younger college set and it was one of this number that suggested Joan should get herself an education and so put herself in a position where she could marry well. Joan had never entered high school, let alone graduated, so she did the obvious thing and bought a fake diploma. Armed with this, and the money she and her mother had been making, she got herself into the exclusive Stephens College. There she proceeded to fail at everything except entertaining the attentive young men of the Phi Delta fraternity to whose house she was the most frequent and popular visitor. This reputation got her blackballed from the sorority houses and her low grades called into question the validity of her high school diploma. Taking discretion as the better part of valour, Joan abandoned hopes of education leading to marriage, and returned to her old way of life in Kansas City.

Joan had one asset and that was a natural ability as a dancer. With the dawn of the Jazz Age she was in her element. She entered contests and regularly won them, which led to her first appearance before a movie camera. She went to work for a seedy company that made stag loops for vending machines. In the first loop she made, aged seventeen, she danced a naked Charleston. Someone told her that there were even bigger bucks to be made in Chicago, so fired with ambition, Joan bought herself a ticket and headed north, arriving in the chilly city with a brand new wardrobe on which she had spent every cent she owned.

Arriving there with nothing but the name of an agent, she made her way to his office only to find it besieged by girls who looked as if they had set up camp there. Joan pushed her way past them all, and forced her way into the agent's office where she burst into tears, threw herself on her knees, sobbed out her plight and begged for work.

That same night Joan made her debut in one of Chicago's sleazier clubs doing a strip three times a night seven nights a week for $20 a week. Figuring that baring all at less than a dollar a throw couldn't be the real reason most of the girls worked there, she discovered that there were private parties at which a clever girl could make a great deal more.

These private shows, popular with the newly enriched bootleggers, expected more from the performers than just dancing, and it was a short step from there to yet another brush with the movie camera.

Throughout her career there were persistent rumours that Joan had made full-blown pornographic movies during her stay in Chicago. She always denied it as a 'vicious rumour'. Her biographers have either glossed over the rumours or dismissed them entirely. The facts are that Joan did make many pornographic films. Mostly these ran less than ten minutes and came into the category of stag reels. They had no production value and their sole selling factor was that they showed a couple, sometimes supplemented by a second girl, performing some variant of the sex act. One, in the possession of the writer, has Joan as an aspirant actress 'auditioning' for a movie producer. Called *The Casting Couch* it has Joan 'nervously' entering the office of the producer who asks, via titles, 'So you want to be an actress?' When Joan nods, no time is wasted on further character development. The producer, complete with handlebar moustache, unbuttons his fly and Joan goes vociferously to work from a kneeling position. A jump cut takes us not to the couch of the title, but to the producer's desk where the now naked Joan shows the producer 'what she's best at'.

This film, plus *Velvet Lips, Coming Home, She Shows Him How* and many other imaginative titles, were to cause Joan much embarrassment over the coming years. On the very night she married Franchot Tone she got a call from a 'collector' telling her that he had a copy of *The Casting Couch* for sale. Joan contacted Louis B Mayer, to whom she had told all, and together they did a deal. It was one of many such deals carried out over the years and it cost some half a million dollars to buy up all 'available copies'. It seems to have occurred to neither of them that movies of this sort are pirated regularly and that it was possible to make endless numbers of copies. Joan tired of the game when one 'collector', having sold what he swore was his last remaining copy, was then found to have others. Someone – surely not Louis B Mayer? – had the man's house burned down.

Hilariously, a snap from this ancient porno turned up in a sixties compilation movie that ran round the world for several years with no one, not even the compilers themselves, realizing that the dark-haired chubby-faced teenager on screen was none other than the 'shocked and disgusted' Joan Crawford herself.

Back in Chicago Joan continued her money-making ways until, aged eighteen, she so impressed J J Schubert, of *The Schubert Review* fame, that he took her from a sex party straight on to a train to New York where she opened on Broadway in his own show, *Innocent Eyes*.

Given a Broadway legitimacy, Joan's social life took off and soon she had as many admirers, but much wealthier ones, as she had had back home in Kansas City.

Legend has it that Joan was discovered by MGM producer Harry Rapf during the run of this show. In fact Harry Rapf never met Joan in New York. Her introduction to MGM came about through Marcus Loew's sharp eye for talent. Loew had just bought into MGM and one night he called on old friend Nils Granlund, a night club owner, who just happened to be entertaining a naked Joan on his office couch. Loew managed to prevent his natural shock and embarrassment from clouding his professional eye and immediately suggested that Joan should take a screen test for MGM at their New York studio. The arrangements for this were obviously complicated since they occupied the two for several nights of fervent discussion before the test date was fixed.

Joan was an immediate success with both test director and crew. In fact, she was so popular that they kept calling her back to make more. Unfortunately the West Coast had not had the opportunity of experiencing her full range and so kept turning her down. Joan went on making tests until even she began to suspect that they'd long ago stopped using film in the camera.

Her social life continued at its hectic pace until one morning she woke to find herself pregnant. A badly botched abortion followed which left Joan incapable of ever having children of her own.

Joan went home to Kansas City to rest and recover while a guilty Nils Granlund used his considerable influence with Marcus Loew to revive MGM's interest in Joan.

Enter Harry Rapf. He looked over the many tests which had come out of New York. Still unable to see what Loew was talking about he called him. Loew referred him to Nils Granlund who told Rapf why he thought they 'owed the girl something'. Rapf sent for her, and Joan, startled to get a call in Kansas City, packed her bags for Hollywood.

Joan spent every available cent on a new wardrobe and got on the train west completely broke. Arriving at MGM determined to be a success she brought her movie *The Casting Couch* to fruition with such enthusiasm that although she made few actual appearances on screen, her contract renewals were never in doubt. For the most part, unencumbered with work, she set about establishing a world record for winning prizes for dancing the Charleston, then a contest rage. She got sixty or so silver cups and a reputation for being the most willing starlet in Hollywood. Such qualifications will do a girl good somewhere down the line. She started getting bit parts and in 1925 she got the ingenue role in *Old Clothes*. This featured-player status, she decided, required that she acquire a house of her own. Having no money she took her problem to the top – Louis B Mayer. Forcing her way through a phalanx of secretaries she got into Louis B's office and poured out her heart-rending story. She had found 'the darlingest sweetest little house' on Roxbury Drive going for the song sum of $18,000 and she 'just had to have it'. The only problem was that she didn't have a cent. Mayer gave due thought to the problem and closed the doors between himself and the eagerly listening staff outside, and went into details with Joan. Emerging a half hour later, flushed of face and smiling, he ordered his secretary to call the treasurer and have a cheque drawn in favour of Joan.

Joan repaid Mayer's generosity with regular visits to his office and, shortly thereafter, her career took off. Billy Cassin had long ago been abandoned in favour of a new name – more fitted to a stripper, Lucille LeSueur, but hardly suitable for Louis B Mayer's rising starlet. He announced a fan contest to find a new name. Someone won with the suggestion of Joan Crawford and she was relaunched with this name on a career that was to span another fifty years.

Mayer had the plumpish Miss Crawford put on a strict diet, had her back teeth removed to give shape to her face, and some drama coaching. There were to be many changes over the years but Joan never lost faith in the casting couch as the way to get the parts she wanted.

Having played nothing but mindless chorus girls on the make, she took direct action when she spotted a meatier role in a picture being set up by producer Hunt Stromberg, who had almost decided on Clara Bow for the part Joan wanted. Joan, as was now her habit, brushed aside such niceties as appointments and secretaries and went directly into Stromberg's office where she, with a confidence born out of her regular visits with Mayer, started shouting that she was the only girl to play in *Dancing Daughters*. In order that Stromberg could better appreciate the magnitude of her talents she took off her clothes and went to work as she had never before. Stromberg allowed himself a moment to recover before informing her that in fact the decision was in the hands of director Harry Beaumont. 'Where's his office?' demanded Joan, barely pausing to get her clothes back on.

Joan got the part and was a tremendous success. It confirmed her view that the way to a good part was through a man's susceptibilities. Harry Beaumont was one of the first recipients of the Joan Crawford method of influencing people, but down the years she was to repeat it with all her directors – some of whom hadn't even been born when she started out!

The stories about her depravations upon defenceless males are legion but some are worth repeating if only to prove that a good idea remains a good idea forever.

Harry Cohn, who ran Columbia, liked to make strife between his stars and producers on the principle of divide and conquer. Hearing that there had been disputes between Crawford and producer Bill Dozier over the making of *Harriet Craig*, Harry called Joan to add fuel to the fire. 'Why doesn't Bill Dozier like you?' he asked her.

'Not like me?' asked Joan sweetly. 'But he does like me. In fact he just said I was sensational. Would you like to have a word with him?' Joan passed the phone to Dozier next to her in bed, but a frustrated Cohn had already hung up.

Having turned down the Deborah Kerr part in *From Here To Eternity* because she didn't like the wardrobe, Joan, now forty-seven, didn't want to lose *Torch Song*. She called the assigned director, Charles Walters, at home. 'I'm coming over with the script and dinner,' she told him. Joan arrived shortly thereafter with a festive picnic basket, adorned in her most glittering jewellery and an incongruously dowdy housecoat. 'I just thought,' she told him, 'that you should have an opportunity to see what you have to work with.' So saying she shed the housecoat to reveal herself wearing nothing at all underneath. Embarrassed, Walters thanked her politely and moved the startled Joan out of the door. She protested every inch of the way. 'But I've got the smallest ass in the business. All the girls at Metro are jealous because I take the smallest size panties – I'm not wearing any right now, but . . .' All to no avail.

So worried was Joan by the rare rejection of her 'sure fire' way with directors and producers that she drank heavily throughout the picture and had to be persuaded to leave her dressing room with the promise of large glasses of vodka.

After co-starring with her in *Johnny Guitar* Sterling Hayden commented: 'There isn't enough money in Hollywood to tempt me into making another picture with Joan Crawford.'

Her director, Nicholas Ray, added, 'As a human being Miss Crawford is a very fine actress.'

With age diminishing her talent Crawford's schedule started showing larger and larger gaps. *Whatever Happened To Baby Jane* brought a brief revival but she was dropped in favour of Olivia de Havilland for its sequel, *Hush, Hush, Sweet Charlotte*.

Accepting a TV half-hour in the *Night Gallery* series she found that her scheduled director was a name unknown to her. Joan, now aged sixty-five, but undaunted, followed her usual procedure in such matters. She called up the director and invited him out to her house for a discussion opportunity. Joan set the stage by filling the entire house with soft candlelight, dressed in a negligee that concealed little, and promised much, and rushed to answer the door at the appointed hour. Throwing it wide open she found a tremulous twenty-year-old Steven Spielberg – on his first directorial assignment – standing there looking at the Hollywood Legend open-mouthed. Joan immediately assumed he was some kind of delivery boy and was astonished to learn that he was her director. Even Joan could recognize the incongruity of trying to seduce a boy young enough to be her great-grandson and so allowed the evening to continue in mutual embarrassment before going to her chaste bed to contemplate the changing times.

There has to be a lot of sympathy for any girl who had the start Joan Crawford did. It made her tough enough to cope with all that Hollywood could throw at her. She used the casting couch and played it for all it was worth, and triumphed where many others had been destroyed. She didn't invent the system any more than she had any choice. We could forgive her much but for the sadistic bringing-up of her adopted children. Her own suffering as a child might have given her a more sympathetic approach.

Joan Crawford had a small talent but she was undoubted Queen of Hollywood for longer than anyone else is ever likely to be.

5

The Thirties – 'We're in the Money'

The thirties was the decade of the big battalions: MGM, Twentieth Century-Fox, Warners and RKO. Close behind came Columbia, United Artists, Universal and, more modestly, Republic. These were the names that were to live and become familiar to audiences through to the present day. The multiplicity of independents were pushed out, with honourable exceptions like Goldwyn and David Selznick, simply because the big names controlled the cinema chains in which the product could be sold.

The coming of sound and the deadly swathe it had cut through the high-priced talent of the silent era largely overshadowed another technical innovation: the development of a Panchromatic film stock. This stock called for far less harsh lighting to be used in the studios and had a greater range of tonal values. It proved far more flattering to actors' faces and brought a whole new and longer lease of life to established stars. It also ended the need to scour the country for precociously developed thirteen-year-olds to play femmes fatales.

Outside Hollywood, in the real world, the Depression that arose after the Wall Street Crash left Hollywood almost unscathed. What precious dollars there were left to the majority of citizens they happily spent to escape their predicament in a few hours of fantasy in a movie house. The Depression led to an even greater influx of hopeful young talent to Hollywood than ever before. Families whose breadwinner was out of a job now looked to their prettiest daughters to go west to salvage something of the family fortunes. These new arrivals were even more desperate than their sisters of an earlier age and in more of a mind to rush into the snares and traps set out for the unwary than avoid them.

So great did this influx become that the Hollywood Chamber of Commerce took paid advertising in thousands of small-town papers desperately trying to stem the flow with awful stories about the very few people that made it in Hollywood and the terrible things that could happen to those that didn't. 'YOU MIGHT HOPE FOR FAME AND FORTUNE BUT FIND ONLY MISERY AND HEARTBREAK' was the depressing message. The girls still came, thinking it wouldn't happen to them. Mostly it did and, even to those that made it through to the magical long-term contract, times had changed. The Moguls, having cleansed their stables, were determined never again to get caught with high-priced talent so rich it was out of control. The newcomers would be lucky to be offered contracts at $50 a week with all the options on the side of the studio. After months, even years, of striving to get their longed-for contract, they could still find themselves dropped after six months. If they managed to make it and become public names they would find that the terms of the contract would be strictly adhered to. A girl might become a star only to find that she was earning little more than her hairdresser and even less than her dressmaker. They would then be further enslaved to the studio by 'loans' with which to buy the trappings of stardom. Step out of line and you were not only in trouble with the studio but also the law. Your house, your car, even your clothes could be repossessed. The Moguls had started to rule by fear. Contract artistes were also now required to report to the studio every day even if there was no work scheduled. To keep them busy they had to attend various classes to develop their talents. These classes were held at most of the studios and it wasn't long before the terrified contract girls found they were also expected to be on call for promotional and social duties. These 'duties' often included entertaining East Coast executives travelling without their wives, and anyone else the studio wanted to impress.

While there was nothing new about the Moguls using sex to persuade those in need of persuasion, what was new was that the girls had little choice. Any girl who showed reluctance to respond to such calls would be listed as 'uncooperative'. Her name would go to the bottom of the list of those available for casting and to the top of the list of those whose options would be dropped. Any girl who got dropped would need very powerful friends indeed to get inside the door of another studio. Usually a dropped option meant oblivion. The girls, for the most part, stayed in line. It wasn't long before the Moguls started regarding their quiescent contract girls as a company harem.

The extreme example of this was Howard Hughes.

Jean Harlow was the first and foremost of Hughes' discoveries. Hughes had financed and produced *Hell's Angels*, a picture which combined his two loves – beautiful women and flying – just as sound was coming in. His leading lady, Greta Nissen, played the part of the girl who provided down-to-earth relaxation for the flyers. The problem with *Hell's Angels* was that it had been shot silent. The very expensive flying sequences could be saved with the addition of effects, but the more down-to-earth action, Hughes decided, would have to be reshot with dialogue. Greta Nissen was a very beautiful lady but no one could get her to speak comprehensible English. Hughes needed a replacement – quick and cheap.

Jean Harlow was then working as an extra on the Hal Roach lot, but previously had worked on two Clara Bow pictures, *Wings* – another story about flyers in France –

and *Wild Party*. These were the last of Clara Bow's pictures as an undisputed star, and it is almost as if fate was giving Jean the chance to pick up the baton from Clara. Her subsequent life so closely resembles Clara's as to be uncanny.

Jean Harlow was born Harlean Carpenter in Kansas City. Shortly after her birth her mother divorced her dentist husband and later married a reputed small-time gangster Marino (Monty) Bello. Jean was to complain to a friend in later years that her life after eleven was 'hell on earth' because Marino was always pawing her. There may have been some truth to this because her mother sent her away to a boarding school. There Jean was often in trouble, mostly for not wearing underwear. Reproved for her well-developed and untrammelled breasts, she told her principal that when she wore a brassiere she couldn't breathe. At sixteen she avoided going home for the summer by running off and marrying the eighteen-year-old son of a local wealthy stockbroker, Charles McGrew. His family were incensed and Jean was afterwards certain that her stepfather had been paid to join the McGrews in an action to get the marriage declared invalid.

Whatever the truth the Bellos immediately moved to Hollywood. Bello used what connections he had to get Jean started around the studios and she suffered many lectures from him about what a girl had to do to get on in the movies.

In a spirit of rebellion, and having developed a temporary aversion to sex, Jean played it straight and, refusing all offers of the couch, continued on as an extra until a fateful day on the Hal Roach lot.

Jean had, in common with every other attractive extra, heard the one about the screen test that could lead to 'big things'. She treated Hughes' minions' approaches with caution until taken to meet Hughes himself. Hughes, fascinated since infancy by women with big breasts, wanted her tested for *Hell's Angels*. She went home to her parents with the big news. Marino was ecstatic. Now, he told her, you have to forget all your small-town ideas. This is the Big Time. Mr Hughes you have to treat with respect. This was Marinoese for saying 'yes' when the question of sex came up. Jean said 'yes' and Hughes said 'yes' and Jean was into *Hell's Angels*. Hughes even took over the direction himself when he was unsatisfied with the way things were going.

The story of a young girl leaping from one young flyer's bed to another, in figure-clinging gowns attesting to the fact that she wore nothing underneath, created a stir with the public. The movie was a success and Harlow an instant star. Other studios started clamouring for Hughes to loan Jean out. Hughes' contract had her at $250 a week but he started loaning her out at first $1500 then $1750 a week. No man is so wealthy that he cannot get greedy. For her $250 a week Jean had to report for regular humiliation from Hughes and was warned against involving herself with any others.

This resulted in some curious stories starting the rounds about Hollywood's newest star. Louis B Mayer was the first to get her on loan-out for a gangster story, *The Secret Six*. On Jean's first day on the lot he summoned her to his office. As she walked in he was holding up a beautiful floor-length white mink and made clear that all she had to do to wear this was to shed what she was already wearing and greet her new 'boss' as befitted a grateful new star. Jean turned on her heel and walked out without even saying a word. Mayer, stunned, might well have been the source of the first rumours that Harlow was 'cold as ice'. As she was again lent out, to Warners, as a hard-boiled gangster's moll, and to Twentieth Century-Fox for *Goldie*, the stories mounted. She was a lesbian. She was asexual. She only did it with dogs! She was a man in drag!! Darryl Zanuck was the man to break through the rumours to the truth. Zanuck, as we shall show in a later chapter, had good reasons to be fascinated by ash-white blondes. He also believed that all women were, at base, whores, and treated Jean accordingly. Curiously Jean responded and in spite of, or because of, all the stories circulating about her, seems to have made a fetish out of greeting Zanuck with friendly four-letter endearments to which he replied in kind, If ever two people seemed anxious to publicize their affair then it was Harlow and Zanuck.

It was after *Platinum Blonde* had established her status, in 1931, that MGM approached Hughes for her contract. Mayer had watched her develop into a genuine star and was still rankled at her cold rejection of him. MGM got her contract for $60,000 and options for Hughes to use her in the future for two pictures at a regular salary.

It was there that she met an MGM executive, Paul Bern. Bern was then working as assistant to the legendary but sickly Irving Thalberg. Bern was generally regarded as Thalberg's successor and due for great things.

To everyone's great surprise hard-boiled sexy Jean married quiet reflective 'everybody's friend' Bern, on 2 July 1932. Jean was twenty-one and Bern was forty-three. On 5 September 1932 Bern killed himself in Jean's bedroom and the rumour mill went into overdrive.

Bern had written a note:

Dearest Dear,
  Unfortunately this is the only way to make good the frightful wrong I have done you, and to wipe out my abject humiliation. You understand that last night was only a comedy.
  Paul.

Bern shot himself through the head with a .38 calibre automatic, which is the only fact that everyone is agreed upon. The generally accepted story is that Paul Bern had been impotent and, weighed down with the guilt of not being able to consummate his marriage to America's number one sex symbol, had shot himself. This story was always hotly denied by Harlow herself and the news of Bern's impotence came as a great surprise to many ladies in and around Hollywood who knew that Bern was 'weird' – according to one lady, he preferred masturbating over her naked body to actual intercourse – but certainly not incapable or impotent. It is certainly strange that it took Bern two months to realize that he couldn't consummate the marriage and even stranger that Jean Harlow should share his bed while he tried. Jean, at the time, was much given to running to her mother whenever anything went wrong in her life, but didn't do so until the night of Bern's suicide.

What then? A famous director, a contemporary of Bern's has another story. The truth according to this man was that Bern was already married when he went through the ceremony with Jean and had been forced to tell her the truth on the night she left for her mother.

The marriage was to a New York actress, Dorothy Millette, and was legally recognized even though there had been no formal ceremony. The legality of the marriage arose from a law, then prevailing, that a cohabitation of more than five years constituted a common law marriage on a par with a marriage created by a formal ceremony. Paul and Dorothy had lived together for many years, with no reports of potency problems, until Dorothy was struck down by a schizomatic amnesia, resulting in her failure to recognize Paul or anyone else. Bern put her into a clinic for treatment and paid the bills over the next ten years. He received regular reports on Dorothy's condition which suggested she would never recover.

During those years Paul had established himself in Hollywood where his reputation grew as a good friend to many women, counselling them, helping them out financially when needed, and only playing out his curious sexual games. During that time his memories, or hopes, of Dorothy faded to the point where he felt confident that he could marry Harlow with impunity.

Unknown to Paul it was his marriage and the resulting headlines which led to Dorothy recovering, if not her mind, then her memory. She wrote to Paul at MGM and in the letter told him that she was coming to Hollywood to 'straighten things out'. Shocked by this letter from a ghost, Paul panicked. His entire future was ruined if he exposed Jean Harlow, MGM's newest star, to the public ignominy of being the victim of a bigamous marriage.

The night that Dorothy was due to arrive in Hollywood Paul told Jean everything. Jean, having had one marriage annulled, was now faced with a second humiliation. The news that America's reigning sex queen was bigamously married could have ended her career. It would certainly be curtains for Paul. Jean left Paul that night, telling Bern that either he buy off Dorothy or forget he'd ever met her.

Dorothy arrived at the house that night. Neighbours were later to speak of a heavily veiled woman stepping out of a chauffeured limousine and hurrying into the house, then of raised voices in heated argument. Soon afterwards the woman hurried from the house and the limousine took off in 'a great hurry'. Within an hour Bern shot himself.

His body was found the next day by his butler who, after recovering from his initial hysteria, called, as any well-trained Hollywood butler would, not the cops but MGM; not only Louis B Mayer but his right-hand man Thalberg and Howard Strickland, then head of Public

Relations for MGM. All three men had cause to remember the shooting of William Desmond Taylor just ten years before, and the effect it had on the careers of Mary Miles Minter and Mabel Normand, and so spent three hours combing the house and removing anything that might affect Jean Harlow. Louis B found Bern's note and handed it to Strickland who was asked to divine its meaning, and, if possible, construct a story around it that would save Harlow.

When the cops were finally called the note was firmly concealed in Mayer's pocket, since they had decided to portray the shooting as by an unknown intruder, as Zukor had done in the case of William Desmond Taylor.

Local enquiries from the neighbours soon turned up the information that Harlow and Bern had been heard arguing and that Harlow had left the house the night before. This, added to the sighting of the heavily veiled woman and further argumentative voices, plus one neighbour who 'positively' identified the veiled woman as Jean Harlow, led the police to conclude that Jean had murdered Bern. This was the worst possible interpretation for Mayer and he hastily produced the note. Suicide was confirmed by the pathologist on the spot as the most likely explanation and the warrant for Jean Harlow was cancelled. Mayer turned to Strickland. What story could they construct that would save Jean? They couldn't let the world believe that Bern had been cheating on Harlow within two months of their marriage. They couldn't allow the world to know that Harlow had been bigamously married. It was then that the story of Bern's impotence was started. They called for supporting evidence from Bern's doctor who would only, guardedly, say that Bern was 'less than well developed' which is a long way from saying he was impotent.

The lie was half round the world, and is still current

today, before Dorothy Millette, the greatest danger to both the story and Harlow's career, was found drowned in the Sacramento River.

Was it all worth while? It certainly was. Harlow's career took off and, for the first time in her life, she started getting good notices from previously cynical critics. Her salary went from $1500 to $5000 a week.

The willingness of Hollywood to feed off its own carrion is strikingly illustrated by two of the movies which Harlow was to make. *Blonde Bombshell* was about a sexy Hollywood star who is ruthlessly exploited by both family and studio when all she wants to do is settle down and have a family. This so closely paralleled Harlow's own life that it must have been painful for her to play out in fantasy what was happening in her own life. Showing all the depth of feeling and sensitivity for which Mayer was famous, they next starred her in *Reckless* in which she plays a showgirl whose husband commits suicide over her affair with another man, William Powell. Powell was conducting just such an affair with Harlow at the time and the studio confidently expected them to marry before the film's release. That was never to be. The effect of Bern's suicide on Harlow was profound. She went totally out of control. She embarked on a series of self-punishing humiliating escapades. Disguising her platinum blonde hair she would cruise bars and pick up men and take them off to ratty hotels where she would lock herself up for days on end while the studio frantically searched for her. A cab driver she hired in Hollywood was told to drive to Tijuana just over the Mexican border. Jean spent four days in bed with the man, who kept telling her she was so like Jean Harlow that she ought to try getting a job as her double!

Jean was to marry again, to cameraman Hal Rosson, but that marriage went the way of all her relationships. Jean at the age of twenty-six suddenly collapsed with, possibly, uraemic poisoning. Mama, being a Christian Scientist, insisted on substituting prayer for medical attention and Jean signed out.

One footnote to the whole episode of the Harlow/Bern marriage came from a man who was employed as darkroom technician to the photographer who took the wedding pictures. He took one look at the developed proofs and called in the photographer. He looked at the blown up prints of the bride and groom and called Bern to explain the problem. The combination of Harlow's thin wedding dress, strong sunlight and her habit of never wearing underwear had resulted in bridal pictures which left nothing to the imagination. Bern asked that they be retouched to save the bride's blushes. He then made a remark which in the light of later events can only be described as poignant: 'After all, it isn't something we'd want to show our grandchildren, is it?'

Harlow's self-punishing promiscuity damaged both her psyche and her health but through it all she showed, on screen, a shining talent for comedy that deserved longer to mature and flower. She certainly deserved to outlive her many exploiters.

Louis B Mayer, the central figure in the Bern/Harlow scandal, carefully projected the image of a family man with great reverence for the role of motherhood. He, an ex-New York street fighter, knocked down both Erich von Stroheim and Jack Gilbert when they made derogatory remarks about women. He sought to further this paternal image by establishing on the MGM lot a school for the young talent he was nurturing for future stardom. Many future stars did emerge from this pool of talent – Ann Rutherford, Mickey Rooney, Bonita Granville, Jane Withers, Lana Turner and, first and foremost, Judy Garland.

Judy was the one to suffer most under Mayer's 'paternal' eye. Every aspect of Judy's life came under Mayer's personal scrutiny but the most depressing for Judy was his insistence that she lose weight. Judy was carrying perfectly normal puppy fat at the time but for Mayer it was an affront to his image of her. She was put on a strict, almost starvation, diet, and had to eat it at Mayer's table in the commissary. An unrelenting diet of chicken soup led Judy to desperate measures and she called in the help of her fellow 'future stars' who proved sympathetic. Among others, Mickey Rooney and Ann Rutherford would climb the studio walls to bring in food for Judy. This sympathetic, and risky, clandestine act of kindness only made matters worse for Judy since, when it was reported that she was still not losing weight, Mayer cut her diet even further and, ominously, added appetite-suppressant drugs to her regime. Many attribute Judy's later problems with drugs to this beginning under the 'benign' eye of Mayer.

In the light of the incandescent talent that came from Judy you might be forgiven for thinking that Mayer was justified by the end if not the means. Judy didn't see it that way. During a concert tour of England someone mentioned Mayer's name in her dressing room. Judy rounded angrily: 'Don't ever mention that pervert's name to me! I still get nightmares over what that man did to me!' Other girl-child recipients of Mayer's paternal interest complained of his habit of putting his arm round them while his hand sought out and fondled their breasts.

Some explanation of Mayer's fondness for harassing his younger starlets may lie in his curious shyness. He must be the most rejected Mogul in the entire history of Hollywood. Many of the ladies he pursued told how he could be put down with a cutting remark. Mayer, the tyrant, was often reduced to tears by rejection. When Jean Howard came into his life he desperately wanted her and entered into an elaborate plan to get her – not as mistress but as his wife. He was at that stage married, but had plans to divorce. Jean Howard was to be the new Mrs Mayer. Had Jean Howard known this at the time she would probably have run a mile: she was at the time conducting a feverish affair with the man she later married, agent Charles Feldman. Mayer employed instead an obscure writer, Ethel Borden, as go-between. Borden was broke and desperately needed Mayer's approval. She was certain that if Jean Howard could be persuaded to return Mayer's affections her own future at the studio would be assured.

Jean Howard was astonished when she learned that Mayer was stricken with love for her. Miss Howard was to say later, 'If he'd have asked I would have gone to bed with him, but marry him – !?' For the moment, though, she was talked into going with Ethel Borden to meet Mayer in Paris where he was on a trip with his sickly wife Margaret. Jean arrived at Le Havre to be met by the anxious Mayer. Mayer started on about how his wife had agreed to a divorce and that now 'nothing stood in the way'. A confused Jean Howard travelled on to Paris, and then was hardly in her room before receiving a message that Mayer wanted to see her urgently. Determined that now was the time to tell him that she had no intention of marrying him, Jean was somewhat taken aback to find Mayer in a towering rage. He had a report on her affair with Charles Feldman, of which neither had made any secret, and was threatening suicide if she told him it was true. Jean told him it was, and Mayer went berserk and, not very seriously, made as if to throw himself out of the hotel window. He was restrained. Jean was sent back to New York on the next boat, and married Charles Feldman. For years afterwards Feldman was barred from doing business on the MGM lot.

This Paris trip was to have another effect on Mayer. Still smarting from Howard's 'betrayal', he found himself being pursued by an Austrian actress, one Hedy Kiesler. Hedy had the previous year made a film called *Ecstasy* in which she had caused a sensation by a prolonged scene in which she first swam naked and then ran through a forest, still naked, to fondle a white stallion with what can only be described as Freudian symbolism. Shortly after its completion she married an Austrian millionaire, Fritz Mandel, who tried to buy up all available copies of the film since he didn't want to share his bride's body with the world. Despairing of this futile exercise Fritz divorced Hedy and settled $250,000 on her as a parting gift. Using her new-found wealth to promote herself Hedy headed for London where an agent introduced her to Mayer. Outwardly puritan, Mayer thought Hedy's appearance in *Ecstasy* just too much for a studio with a family image like his own and rejected her. Hedy was undeterred. She bought a ticket aboard the *Normandie*, on which Mayer was returning to the States, and engineered constant meetings with him on board. By the end of the six-day crossing Mayer had come not only to reassess Hedy's talents but had confirmed his opinion with a contract backed by a star-building campaign. He had also passed on the ill-fated Barbara LaMarr's name to her in the hope that it would lessen the impact of his new star having played a full-frontal nude.

Mayer's caution over Hedy Lamarr, as she was now known, was due to the revival of the long-moribund Hay Code. This resurrection of 'moral awareness' had been brought about by two, on the surface quite disparate, Hollywood phenomena: Mae West and Busby Berkeley.

Nudity was nothing new in Hollywood films and dated back to 1916 when Annette Kellerman and June Caprice had both appeared nude. There had been nudes galore in

Birth of a Nation and *Intolerance*. Betty Blythe had played *The Queen of Sheba* bare breasted in 1924, and de Mille had Claudette Colbert taking a nude bath in *King of Kings. Ben Hur* had one scene, not shown in the US, which was positively overflowing with bare-breasted teen-age extras. De Mille got under the wire with the heavy religious tone of his films, while Busby Berkeley's blatant use of the female anatomy as nothing more than a casual decorative element to his spectacular musical numbers aroused the ire of the censors. Off-screen Berkeley was even more outrageous. His chorus girls were subject to an iron discipline from bi-sexual Berkeley. He expected them, like Sennett's Bathing Beauties, to appear at his social parties where they soon earned a reputation that paled their wildest routines on screen into insignificance. For a girl to refuse or attempt to avoid such a Command Performance was considered to be tantamount to resigning from the famed line-up. One graduate of the Berkeley mill, Betty Grable, talked about her early days. Betty started in the chorus at the age of thirteen and saw Hollywood from the bottom to the top. 'Those parties were the pits. You'd come out in the early dawn feeling like a piece of meat dogs had been fighting over all night. If my mother hadn't been with me I'd have killed myself a dozen times over. A lot of girls did. It was soul-destroying but everywhere you turned there were people, agents, lawyers, casting directors, telling you stories about how so-and-so made it that way. The message was that either you played their game their way or you got out of town. It haunted everyone even when they became stars. There was always someone who knew you when you were crawling in dirt and begging for a break. One short cut was to marry an already established star. I nearly did once but his pals laughed me out of the frame on account of how young I was and how many times I'd been round the

Right: A star is born: Carl Laemmle's advertisement in *The Moving Picture World* in March 1910, coyly announcing his acquisition of Florence Lawrence, formerly 'the Biograph Girl'

We Nail a Lie

The blackest and at the same time the silliest lie yet circulated by enemies of the "Imp" was the story foisted on the public of St. Louis last week to the effect that Miss Lawrence (the "Imp" girl, formerly known as the "Biograph" girl) had been killed by a street car. It was a black lie because so cowardly. It was a silly lie because so easily disproved. Miss Lawrence was not even in a street-car accident, is in the best of health, will continue to appear in "Imp" films, and very shortly some of the best work in her career is to be released. We now announce our next films:

"The Broken Bath"
(Released March 14th. Length 950 feet.)

A powerful melodrama dealing with a young chap, his sweetheart and a secret society. There's action from the first foot of film and it keeps you five million miles up in the air until the happy finale. This is the kind of film dozens of our customs have been begging us to produce. Watch for it.

"The Time-Lock Safe"
(Released March 17th. Length 960 feet.)

A drama that suddenly and unexpectedly turns into a farce. If your little child were locked in a safe and you paid a professional safe-blower a stack of money to get him out, and then found the kid safely ensconced in the towel basket and not in the safe at all, would you be glad or would you be sore? Imagine what a corking good picture can be worked up on this plot.

If you never do another thing in your life, get "Mother Love" (released March 7th). It's our film d'pippereno!

Independent Moving Picture Co. of America
111 East 14th St., New York, Carl Laemmle, Pres.

Left: Mack Sennett, proud possessor of Hollywood's first and busiest casting couch

The Sennett Studios at Edendale – 'no starlet unlaid'

A Sennett harem. Attendance at the boss's orgies was compulsory

Right: Carl G. Laemmle (second from left) with Mary Pickford

Left: Marion Davies. Graduating from the Ziegfeld couch, she fell off a bicycle into a heap of Hearst money

Lewis J. Selznick's first signing, Clara Kimball Young

Harry Cohn, dapper head of Columbia and master of the casting couch

Louise Brooks, a new
kind of woman

Jesse Lasky and
Adolph Zukor,
pioneers of casting

Opposite above: Jean Harlow with husband Paul Bern

Opposite below: Harlow and husband-to-be Hal Rossen meet the press

Above: Barbara La Marr, 'the girl that was too beautiful', with Frank Mayo. La Marr liked her lovers like roses – by the dozen

Right: Clara Bow, devotee of football teams

Right: Joan Crawford (right) looks forward, her porn movie career behind her

Above: Marlene Dietrich in her early German career ...

...and after, the ultimate sophisticate

Loretta Young (right) with mother and sisters

Above: MGM 'daddy' Louis B. Mayer with his 'family'

Left: Carole Landis, the 'studio hooker'

Right: Lupe Velez, Hollywood's favourite party girl

Below: Sam Goldwyn (left) greets Broadway boss Florenz Ziegfeld on arrival in L.A., 1929

Gene Tierney, Rita
Hayworth's rival for Ali
Khan

Bella Darvi with
Kirk Douglas in
1955, a decade
after her Gestapo
ordeal

Above: Darryl Zanuck with Juliette Greco – still swinging in the sixties!

Right: Zanuck, bruised by his European excursions (he claimed it was an old ski wound)

Left: Zanuck, waiting to pounce on Dorothy Dandridge

Below: Jane Russell in her most famous pose

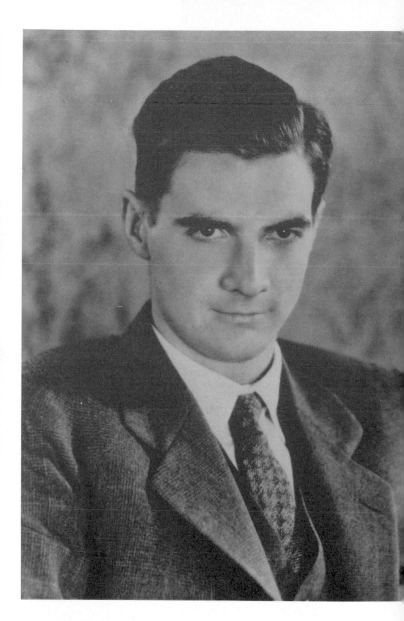

Howard Hughes

The tragic Marilyn Monroe

track. You have to remember that I was little more than a kid. That is, if ever I was a kid!'

One aspirant to the Hollywood mill was much less fortunate than Betty but, in some ways, her name lives on with never a book written about Hollywood that doesn't mention her. Lillian (Peg) Entwhistle was a young but already successful actress when she left London to try her fortune in Hollywood. Having London stage credits and approving critical notices to her name, she imagined that talent was enough. She soon found that London could be outer Siberia for all Hollywood cared. Peg soon found that she was starting again all over. Failing to impress any of the established agents and running short of money she joined an agency known as Starr Agency which then had offices on Gower Street. This was no 'talent' agency in the normal sense of the word. Their speciality was delivering girls to order for Hollywood parties where she, and others, were assured they stood the best chance of being 'noticed'. Realizing that she was becoming no more than a paid party girl, Peg tried the other accepted methods of getting noticed. First she had a series of 'pin-ups', then full nudes taken. These pictures were more likely to be seen by surfeited casting directors than the more conventional portraits, she was told. When that didn't result in anything but a few sweaty afternoons on couches, she was persuaded that the 'sure-fire' method was to make a stag reel movie. The theory was that to approach someone like, say, Darryl Zanuck, and get him to see some footage on an unknown girl was asking too much of a busy executive. To approach him with a 'sensational stag reel of a girl that does everything and'll make your hair curl' was thought to ensure that the girl would be seen. If the goodies on display were as good as hoped the executive might then ask for a face-to-face which was more likely to be belly-to-belly, but never mind. That was the way it was done, Peg was told.

Peg Entwhistle went through the motions and the reels were made. All that happened was more sticky afternoons on the couch and the usual 'we'll be in touch'.

Sickened by what she had done with a promising career Peg took herself to the top of the 'Hollywood' sign that dominated Hollywood, and still does today, and threw herself from the top to her death on the rocks below. Unknown to herself she was blazing a trail that other girls would follow, and ensuring herself a place in the Hollywood legend.

Being noticed was the most important thing for most of the girls that came to Hollywood. One that came to hide was a girl called Imogene Wilson, who changed her name to Mary Nolan on arrival. Mary needed to hide from a scandal which had broken in New York. Mary had been a Ziegfeld Follies girl when comedian Frank Tinney picked her out of the line-up for his personal pleasure. It was a long-standing tradition at the Follies that the top comedian got first choice of the chorus line-up. Frank had chosen well. Mary and he had a lot in common – a taste for the lesser-trod paths of sado-masochism. Their esoteric affair came to the attention of Frank's wife and she threatened an 'or else' which involved Mary fading from New York. Mary went to Hollywood where, with a change of name, she hoped she wouldn't be noticed. Mary was sensationally beautiful, and those that knew her thought she had a lot of potential talent. Instead of pursuing what chances she might have had she was introduced, through the grapevine, to Hollywood's leading boots and whips players – Wallace Beery, Erich von Stroheim and Lionel Atwill. A true masochist, she was soon moving among the powerful and pursuing her obsessive need for pleasure through pain. Lionel Atwill, as will be shown later, was an English actor who prided himself on his orgiastic parties. Mary was soon a star turn at such gatherings, giving performances which the Marquis de Sade would have been sorry to have missed.

She was, at the same time, getting parts in pictures, and it was the clash of obsession and work which led her into a disastrous course of action that cut her career short. She was cast, largely through the influence of star Wallace Beery, into a good little part in a picture he was scheduled to make. To celebrate Wallace took her and his whips on a celebratory weekend which ended with Mary in hospital and her part in the picture going to someone else. Furious, Mary threatened to sue Beery but the studio heavies moved in on her and advised against it. Instead they suggested she accept $50,000 and leave Hollywood. She did and that was the end of Mary Nolan/Imogene Wilson.

While Erich von Stroheim was an admirer of Mary Nolan's, Josef von Sternberg was not likely to share her sexual tastes. Von Sternberg had the least promising début of any Hollywood director before or since. After years as an assistant director he was given a chance to direct by an English actor. The film was financed by the actor himself and was intended as a showcase for his talents. The extremely low budget created endless problems and the final result was a shaky proposition commercially but was considered to show promise for its director. MGM took him up and his first three pictures for them were all either reshot by someone else or shelved. Von Sternberg was back to acting as other directors' assistants when B P Schulberg at Paramount rescued him and assigned him a pot-boiler gangster movie, *Underworld*. The movie was, to the surprise of everybody, an outstanding hit and von Sternberg's star began to rise. However, it was when he was invited to Berlin to direct a UFA film, *The Blue Angel*, that von Sternberg was to find the star that was to ensure his lasting fame.

Marlene Dietrich had played, with varying success, in

German pictures since 1923. She was long past the age to be discovered when von Sternberg and she met. *The Blue Angel* was an instant success and von Sternberg took his 'discovery' back to Hollywood and Paramount, where, possibly to disguise her true age, he told everyone that he had discovered her in a student play and that *The Blue Angel* was her first film. Marlene seems to have gone along with this to such an extent that she, even today, denies she made any films before *The Blue Angel*. When faced with the indisputable evidence of her previous roles she dismisses them as not counting since they were silents. It is obvious that 'new discoveries' aged thirty were not going to go down well so it was in both their interests to maintain the fiction in those early days. For von Sternberg she was an object of total adoration. Throughout the movies he made with her in Hollywood – *Morocco*, *Dishonoured*, *Shanghai Express*, *The Scarlet Empress*, and *The Devil is a Woman* – he brings loving testimony to his 'goddess'. A master of the visual, von Sternberg all but abandoned plot and simply concentrated his camera, and all eyes, on Marlene.

The worship with which he regarded Marlene on camera was carried through to his private life to such an extent that his wife divorced him, claiming Marlene had alienated his affections.

The 'alienation' fell far short of adultery, however. Marlene on arrival in Hollywood had brought with her the unconventional habits of the Berlin of the twenties – the mannish dress, the smoking in public. Her 'mystery' and sophistication had also attracted a coterie of admirers, including Claudette Colbert and Lila Damita, into what became known as her sewing circle. Members of the sewing circle, in direct contrast to Nazimova's frenzied homosexual circle, were generally acknowledged to be bisexual women. One of the few men admitted to the circle was the adoring von Sternberg who was not above dancing attendance on the ladies when they met. One might wonder why von Sternberg never considered filming Sacher-Masoch's classic study of male masochism, *Venus in Furs*, until we look again at the films he made with Dietrich and conclude that he did! Marlene was always the sophisticated self-confident woman pursued by men in the grip of slavish devotion. Some of the sadistic fantasies imposed upon her character in *The Scarlet Empress* would have as much difficulty with the censors today as they did in 1934. In *The Devil is a Woman* Lionel Atwill's character is openly that of Severin, the central enthralled male in *Venus in Furs*. Von Sternberg insisted on more and more elaborate settings and costumes for his own Venus until Paramount considered he was becoming too obsessive and separated him from Dietrich. Marlene went on to demonstrate her endurance with other directors but von Sternberg's career nose-dived. Bereft of the object of his adoration his chance to re-establish himself came when Korda invited him to Britain to direct Charles Laughton and Merle Oberon in *I, Claudius* which, like his first three films, was abandoned only half finished.

Merle Oberon, the star of the abandoned epic, had come to London from her homeland of India in 1928, aged seventeen. Merle, real name Queenie O'Brien, was of mixed Anglo-Indian parentage – social death in both India and London at the time, and, understandably, Merle sought to hide it. Her first months in London were of dire poverty since she discovered that the 'rich' relative that was supposed to take care of her on arrival turned out to have grossly exaggerated his circumstances in his letters home. Merle had to take some miserable jobs around Soho and did what she had to do in order to get by. One of these miserable jobs was as a lowly film extra. In the British studios of those days an extra was paid just over a pound a day and, if she wanted ever to be called again, was expected to be at the beck and call of the almighty assistant director. Merle did get called again, often. On one of these calls her sloe-eyed beauty was spotted by Leslie Howard who, despite his mild-mannered pipe-smoking screen image, was a girl chaser to exceed even the more flamboyant Errol Flynn. To be 'noticed' by a star was every girl extra's dream, and soon Merle, highly flattered, was moving in far-exalted circles. Howard, not a mean man, brought her to the attention of Alexander Korda, at the time Britain's most successful producer. Merle changed partners, with Howard's blessing, and was rewarded with a Korda contract. Her casting card had the unequivocal message tagged to it: 'AK special interest' which ensured that any director looking for a cast and wishing to ingratiate himself with Korda could do no better than consider Merle. When she played Anne Boleyn in Korda's biggest hit, *The Private Life of Henry VIII*, she attracted the attention of Hollywood and, in particular, Joe Schenck, one of the studio's founders. Her first Hollywood picture was not for MGM but for Twentieth Century-Fox. Her appearance in *Folies Bergère* with Maurice Chevalier was enough to attract a contract from Goldwyn, but even more attention from Joe Schenck, with whom she started an affair. Korda became alarmed when he heard about this, and that it was getting serious, and called her back to London to start the ill-fated *I, Claudius*. She returned and Korda, after many years of keeping her as his mistress, realized that he genuinely loved her and handed her the prize she most wanted – marriage.

As a lowly extra girl and bit player she had first been tested, in London, by Irving Asher, then scouting for Jack Warner. Jack Warner viewed the test and cabled back: 'If

you want to sleep with women go ahead, but don't waste
my money shooting screen tests of them!'

Linda Darnell might never have made it but for her
mother, Pearl. Like so many Hollywood mothers, Pearl
was using her precociously beautiful daughter to act out
her own fantasies. In Dallas, Texas, Linda was being
pushed into modelling by the age of twelve. Photographers took one look at the fully developed figure and
believed her mother when told she was sixteen. When an
unwary talent scout from Fox came into town Pearl was
lying in wait. She rushed the now fourteen-year-old Linda
to his hotel suite, delivered a fifteen-minute harangue on
her daughter's attributes and suitability for stardom
before, without the scout uttering a word, left them alone
'to get to know each other better'. Pearl walked the
blocks for a nail-biting hour before returning to find how
things had gone. She found a white-faced guilty talent
scout demanding to know why Mother hadn't told him
Linda was only fourteen. 'Why should I have?' asked
Momma, adding in mock concern, 'Why? What happened?' The scout murmured some platitudinous compli-
ments on her daughter's potential, and the moment he
had got rid of them packed his bags and was gone from
Dallas before the Sheriff could yell 'statutory rape'.

Pearl was furious. The mouse had had the cheese and
escaped the trap! Taking the bemused Linda by the hand
she pursued the man to the Fox lot in Hollywood. The
frightened scout promised them 'anything' and desperately arranged for Linda to be dropped into the test
schedules. Zanuck's reaction on seeing the test was that
the girl was too young.

Pearl tried again and again and got the same reaction.
'Too developed to play children not old enough to play
women.' Finally admitting defeat, Pearl took little Linda

back home to Dallas where she faced a barrage of ribaldry from her school-friends.

But Pearl never gave up. A year later she entered Linda into a beauty contest whose first prize was a screen test with RKO. Linda won the contest hands down and was duly tested, at RKO, by cameraman Peverell Marley. Marley was thirty-eight, Linda not yet sixteen. Marley took a 'special interest' in the beautiful teenager and during her short visit to Hollywood, squired her around town, encouraged by the anxious Pearl.

RKO's reaction was identical to Zanuck's. Hearing of the negative response from RKO Pearl again packed her bags for Dallas. However, the Peverell connection was to pay off: he moved to Fox and, given an opportunity, ran the old Fox test again for Zanuck, adding additional information of a highly personal nature. This was enough to intrigue Zanuck and he had Linda brought back to Hollywood. Pearl and daughter proved such a hit with Zanuck that he made room for the beautiful sixteen-year-old *and* her mother in his daily schedule. Fox signed this totally inexperienced newcomer to a contract which started at $750 a week. Big money, in 1939, for the daughter of a postal worker. Her father, bemused and unimpressed by the Hollywood ambitions of his wife, reacted by applying for a transfer to Los Angeles, where he continued delivering mail.

Meanwhile Linda was delivering on screen. All Momma's hopes and dreams came true when Linda was tried out in a showcase movie – a vehicle for showing a troupe of new talent in the company of tried and tested stars – and was an immediate hit. Everyone wanted to know who the sultry, busty 'woman' was. Zanuck had, to keep her busy, assigned her a routine quickie Western, but when the reaction cards started rolling in, he pulled her from it to *star* her with Tyrone Power in *Daytime Wife*. Later that year the sixteen-year-old was again playing the sultry grown-up woman in *Stardust*, this time with John Payne. Now Zanuck had a problem. The fan magazines were clamouring for the tiniest details of the new star's life. How were they going to break the news that 'sultry, sexy, screen siren, Linda Darnell' was only sixteen years old? What was good for the more innocent early years of Hollywood was not acceptable in the late thirties. They finally solved their problem by the possibly unique and extraordinary ploy of *adding* two years to her age. Linda herself had been rocketed to stardom so fast that she could barely believe it was happening. That great connoisseur of busty brunettes, Howard Hughes, took an interest in her, and wooed her by inviting her to lunch. Lunch turned out to be in San Francisco whence he flew the startled Linda in his own private plane. Lunch was served, for the two of them, in the vastness of the entire top floor of the luxurious Fairmont Hotel, where they enjoyed nothing less than an intimate banquet. Linda, overwhelmed, supplied dessert. When news of this raid on his personal star reached Zanuck he was furious. He called up Hughes and told him in four letter words to keep his hands off Linda Darnell. Hughes withdrew from the field.

Linda went on to great success in Fox pictures but suffered premature box-office ageing. By the end of the fifties it seemed to moviegoers that she had been around a long time. She was still only in her mid-thirties – her public didn't realize how young she had been when she started, or the exaggeration of her age. At thirty-five she found herself a back number. At forty-two, having suffered a life-long fear of fire, she accidentally set light to herself and thirty-six pain-wracked hours later the precocious child from Dallas was dead.

Most young girls pushed towards a movie career had their mothers as the main impetus. Mary Astor was different in that, born Lucille Langehanke in 1906, she was propelled by the ambitions of her father. He saw no difference between his beautiful child and the reigning screen stars, then Mary Pickford, Blanche Sweet and Lilian Gish. To him they represented the American Dream and he was determined to achieve the same for his daughter. To this end he uprooted his family from Quincy, Illinois and, totally penniless, moved to Chicago, then a centre of film-making. Chicago proved too small a town to appreciate Mary's talents and so he again moved, still penniless, to New York. There he struck up an acquaintance with a photographer, Charles Albin, who arranged a meeting with child fancier D W Griffith. Mary didn't impress, but Father held tenaciously on to Albin who next arranged a meeting with Famous Players-Lasky. They took her on for a six-month contract, gave her some bits and walk-ons, then dropped her. However, Father was encouraged by this and persisted. The harassed Albin got Mary, now fifteen, signed with a company called Tri-Art. There she played two-reelers and learned more about her craft. Mary was next taken, by Father, to meet the dreaded ogre of the couch, Lewis J Selznick. Selznick was impressed enough to give her two good parts, and Mary was starting to believe that she might have a serious career ahead of her. It was then, in New York, that Father got her to see John Barrymore, then playing Broadway with his *Hamlet*, and taking a break from filming. Father figured that a famous actor like Barrymore could have a great deal of influence. Barrymore's reputation as a seducer of very young girls could not have passed Father's notice but he was determined that Mary should be 'somebody' and, by this time, was so desperately enthused that he must have been considering that the means could be safely ignored in the headlong rush to the end: fame and fortune. On their first meeting Father enthused: 'This is a great honour, Mr Barrymore. If you take an interest in Mary then I'm sure we'll do anything to please you.' Barrymore raised his famous eyebrows and intoned, '*We?*'

An arrangement was arrived at where little Mary would be delivered to John Barrymore each afternoon at two P.M. and stay until five for 'special coaching', except on those afternoons when Barrymore had a matinée, of course. The social niceties were observed in so far as mother always accompanied Mary to these coaching sessions, but her chaperonage must have been a little difficult since she took her knitting out on to the terrace of Barrymore's apartment and, no matter the weather, stayed there until called in to take Mary away. Mary herself reported that these coaching sessions always ended with the two of them, Barrymore aged forty and Mary aged fifteen, in bed.

The arrangement paid off for the Langehanke family. Barrymore, for once, genuinely took to his young protégée/mistress and insisted that she play his leading lady in *Beau Brummel* and be paid $1100 for doing so. It was the start of a career that was to carry Mary through more than a hundred movies and six decades of fine performances. One curiosity of the Mary Astor story is that she never wanted to be billed above the title as a full-blown star. She preferred the more secure ground of the featured player which might account for her longevity, but also for the huge scandal that blew up in her face in 1936 when there was no studio to protect her.

Her second husband had divorced her; though this was uncontested by Mary, she decided to fight for her daughter's custody. It was then that her husband, Franklyn Thorpe, a Beverly Hills doctor, introduced into evidence Mary's diaries which detailed her various infidelities in language totally at variance with the ice-cool ladylike persona of her screen image. George S Kaufman had met Mary in New York in 1933. According to the diary their meeting was like oil meeting fire. Extracts read in court included: 'It's been years since I felt a man up in public, but I just got carried away . . .' 'We made love all night long. We were on to our fourth climax when dawn came . . .' 'We flew into each other's arms . . . he was rampant in an instant . . . I was never undressed by anyone so fast in my entire life . . . We sweetly fucked the entire afternoon . . .' The good doctor got his divorce and the diary was burned as pornography. Everyone was confident that this was the end of Mary's career, especially because of Mary's insistence on remaining freelance, but it wasn't. She went on to even greater triumphs for another thirty years. Times were changing. Just the suggestion of impropriety had been enough to end the careers of Mary Miles Minter and Mabel Normand just ten short years previously. The nature of scandal was changing.

Carole Landis was a lady made for Hollywood. She got her first break with Cecil B de Mille, while still attending the Hollywood High School. De Mille had a 'thing' about feet, which he considered one of the more interesting portions of the female anatomy. This is evident in the famed de Mille bathroom scenes where, without fail, the leading lady will lift her dainty foot from beneath the all-concealing bubbles to gently and lovingly soap her legs! Casting a movie for Hal Roach, *One Million Years BC*, de Mille mystified everyone by disappearing with promising girls on to the back lot. Hal Roach followed one at a discreet distance and found de Mille was asking the aspirant girls to show him how they could run bare-foot across broken ground. The one that did it best was Carole Landis and she got the part, which was to lead to brief stardom.

Carole had only previously played bits, including a

chorus girl in *Varsity Show* at Warner's. This had been
directed by Busby Berkeley, and so Carole had already
had her first taste of the Hollywood party scene. Shortly
afterwards Carole married businessman Irving Wheeler,
who took objection to her partying on demand with other
men. He, much bowed by the horns he wore from the
first day of his marriage, selected Busby Berkeley as the
fall guy and sued him for $250,000 for the old stand-by,
'alienating his wife's affections'. Why Irving should have
picked on Busby when he had half Hollywood to choose
from is a mystery, but the suit was, in any case, thrown
out of court. Carole's next move was to the Twentieth
Century-Fox lot where she deposed Alice Faye in the
back room which Darryl F Zanuck kept to 'entertain' his
female contract artistes. Milton Sperling, a Fox producer,
tagged her 'The Studio Hooker' but far from being
offended Carole took to introducing herself that way on
nights when she was detailed to dispel the well-known
loneliness that overtook Fox executives from New York
when they came out to the coast. Carole made a lot of
pictures but never broke through to genuine stardom. She
ended it all with an overdose in 1948 – supposedly for
unrequited love of Rex Harrison. Quite what 'unrequited'
meant in this context has been the source of much
lexicographical research ever since.

If Carole couldn't take it, Lupe couldn't get enough! Lupe
Velez had first come to Hollywood in 1926 when she
played in a Douglas Fairbanks movie, *Gaucho*. There
followed a whole series of 'exotic' parts, in which she
played native girls, Indian girls and sometimes even
Mexican girls. Far more spectacular than anything she
played on the screen was the way in which she stormed
into Hollywood. Lupe was convent-educated until fourteen, when she became the sole supporter of her very
large family. Fabulously beautiful even at that young age,

she soon had many admirers and started work in one of the more exclusive of the border town bordellos.

In Hollywood she went through all the leading men at such a rate that the gossips considered it simpler to name those she hadn't slept with. Running through husbands and lovers she left an exhausted wake behind her wherever she went. She was never absent when a Latin American fighter appeared in Hollywood; she would encourage them by climbing into the ring and dancing a little flamenco in front of them, her skirt revealing that she wore no underwear and carrying the implicit promise of closer inspection should they win their fights! Bored at a party with her husband, Johnny Weissmuller, ex-Olympic swimming champion and on-screen Tarzan, she leapt on to a piano, threw off her clothes and invited anyone who cared to step up for 'a piece of chili'. Weissmuller stuck it out for six years of marital fighting and party gang-banging before calling it a day. Lupe, with her house full of seventy-two canaries and fourteen chihuahuas, hardly noticed.

Everyone looked forward to the traditional end-of-picture party when Lupe was starring. It was a Hollywood habit for the stars to give out gifts to their fellow players and technicians. Lupe often gave herself, down to the last electrician.

Unfortunately, with life at that pace, time has a way of catching up. Soon Lupe was down to playing parodies of her Mexican Spitfire image in low-budget Leon Errol comedy two-reelers.

Finally, broke and pregnant, rejected by her then lover, Lupe decided to end it all. Determined to die as splendidly as she had lived she went to considerable trouble to stage the bed on which she expected to be found. She arranged flowers, candles, and solemn music set to repeat over and over on the phonograph. Arrayed in her very best negligee Lupe swallowed a huge drug overdose and lay down to await the end.

Life, however, had one last trick to play on its most vital member. At some point Lupe's stomach made one violent attempt to stay alive and she started to vomit up the fatal overdose. Lupe must have tried to respond, or maybe she changed her mind, but on the way to the bathroom she fell for the last time and when found, instead of the carefully staged tableau, there was just a mess where Lupe had once been.

Lupe had come to Hollywood to play them at their own game but finally lost. One who triumphed, and never needed the couch to succeed, was Mae West. Mae rode into town on the crest of a series of fighting actions against various public order authorities back East where her stage shows were always being raided for being salacious and immoral. The immorality lay entirely in Mae's raunchy dialogue, and when sound came to Hollywood, so did Mae.

Mae was forty when she made her movie debut, and not needing the couch as a way ahead, she reversed it. No leading man ever got into a Mae West picture without proving that he had what it took to satisfy her. Constantly surrounded by a muscular group of bodyguards – justified, said Mae, by threats on her life – she had as direct a way with men off-screen as on. She had a habit of taking by the hand any man on set that took her eye and leading him directly to her dressing room where she would hang out a sign: 'DO NOT DISTURB – EXCEPT IN CASE OF FIRE'. One recipient of this direct approach, now a retired cameraman, on entering her trailer found three of her muscular bodyguards already there and ready for action. Since Mae obviously had no intention of asking them to go Our Hero, so he says, made his excuses and left.

*   *   *

The story of the making of a movie called *Having a Wonderful Time* so neatly sums up the thirties and its attitudes to the casting couch that we cannot leave it out. *Having a Wonderful Time* was a comedy set in the borscht circuit of the Catskill Mountains, a resort area very popular with the New York Jewish population. Movies on location in the east were very popular with East Coast executives who could count on the assistant directors arranging them some after-hours relaxation Hollywood-style without having the tiring train journey west. On *Having a Wonderful Time* this essential aspect of the scheduling was taken care of by bringing in twenty, count them, top magazine and fashion models from two of New York's top agencies.

The assistant directors, being from Hollywood, assumed the girls would be as pliant as the girls back home would have been in similar circumstances. They hadn't reckoned on the harder-nosed New York model who, unused to getting up that early, also resented the suggestion that she make herself sexually accessible to the RKO executives. Mutiny set in. The models much preferred the younger members of the crew to the ageing executives and started making their own choices. To make matters worse the RKO executives had invited along the head of the bank that was currently supporting them and picked out the most beautiful girl for him. Frustrated at 'his' girl's constant headaches the bank president started grumbling. The RKO executives started getting jumpy, and heads started to roll. Red Skelton, the lead actor, was replaced by Jack Carson. The director was replaced by George Stevens, and the lonely executives, cheated of their 'rights', started to give everyone A TERRIBLE TIME.

The movie was reduced to chaos. The end result when finally cobbled together looked even worse than they had feared. The bank president withdrew his backing and RKO had to find a new studio head.

Having a Wonderful Time was first shelved, and when brought out in the days 'when you could sell anything' – the war years – it managed to be one of the resounding flops in that entertainment-hungry era.

Yet the best of the thirties is still to come. If the heyday of the casting couch was during the confident, prosperous thirties then it was to end with the biggest, widest, longest casting couch of them all. David O Selznick, son of Lewis, was about to cast *Gone with the Wind* and establish movieland's first coast to coast casting couch.

6

Coast to Coast Casting Couch

When David O Selznick bought the rights to *Gone with the Wind* he might have been forgiven for thinking he had reaped a whirlwind. His initial backer was Jock Whitney, but Whitney couldn't bankroll the huge budget necessary. Selznick needed something to whip up public enthusiasm for the movie while he raised the necessary finance. He was finally to come up with the oldest gimmick of all: the search for a 'new face'.

Rhett Butler had been cast by public acclamation: Clark Gable. The juiciest female role of the decade was, however, still open, that of Scarlett O'Hara. It was the casting for this part that was to rouse half Hollywood and finally the nation to something approaching hysteria.

It seemed that almost every woman under the age of forty in the entire United States was half-convinced she could play Scarlett.

One who was *certain* that she could not only play her but *was* Scarlett was the bisexual, tempestuous Tallulah Bankhead. Tallulah came to the theatre and movies from a rich and pampered background and she enjoyed herself and indulged herself to the full. So far as she was concerned she was the only contender. The qualifications she put forward were that she was from the South – Alabama – and she had a 'scarlet' reputation. The fact that she was closing fast on her fortieth birthday she saw as no obstacle. She had had hundreds of highly public love affairs, had a habit of taking her clothes off at parties, was always surrounded by people who liked her cocktail of drugs, alcohol and non-stop sex. In summary

Tallulah believed that life was for living. The other ace she believed she held was that the main backer of the project, Jock Whitney, was her current lover. Tallulah might have had a better Hollywood career but she had most of the Moguls scared into believing that no one could handle her. David O Selznick was no exception but he couldn't afford to rebuff her too positively.

To reinforce her claim Tallulah journeyed to Hollywood and went directly to George Cukor, at the time slated to direct. In the spirit of bisexual solidarity Cukor arranged a test for Tallulah. Since there was, at this stage, no script, he had her read directly from the pages of the novel with himself reading in the cue lines.

Hearing that Selznick had viewed her test without enthusiasm Tallulah tried a different tack. She contacted her family's many influential friends in Alabama and soon had petitions, town meeting resolutions and letters from everybody from the State Governor downwards pouring into Selznick's office. These missives spoke with one voice – Tallulah Bankhead had to play Scarlett.

Selznick started getting desperate. Rhett had been thrust upon him and now it seemed he was about to be buried in the Bankhead avalanche and he still didn't have the money to start the picture. Then salvation came when Tallulah made a false move. She married an actor called John Emery whose only claim to fame was that he looked enough like John Barrymore to fill in when that actor was 'indisposed'. In many Barrymore films the man you see in distant shots or with his back to the camera is not Barrymore, but Emery. This defiant declaration of her heterosexual propensities lost Tallulah a lot of her gay backing. There was even a song in gay bars and meeting places lamenting the event but, even worse for Tallulah, was the offence Jock Whitney took. He withdrew his lobbying for Tallulah and the pressure on Selznick eased dramatically.

This only left the field wide open for every other actress in Hollywood to put in her personal pitch. Loretta Young went to work on Cukor. Miriam Hopkins thought the best route would be through David's agent brother, Myron. Norma Shearer – now without the big-gun support of the late Irving Thalberg – paid for her own screen test and presented it to Selznick in a most unoriginal way: in bed. Selznick was sufficiently impressed to test public opinion on Norma by having an item printed saying that she was 'under active consideration'. The public responded by letting Selznick know that Norma Shearer wasn't what they had in mind.

However, the knowledge that the pulling power of the part he had at his disposal had been enough to bring the former Queen of MGM to bed fired up Selznick's enthusiasm for finding a Scarlett.

Soon the Selznick office was buzzing as both stars and starlets chanced their arm, not to mention the rest of their anatomy, on the chance of playing Scarlett. It became a regular feature of his secretary's day to have some girls come running out of the office complaining, while others walked slower and with satisfied smiles. One of the former was Evelyn Keyes. Pert and shapely she went into Selznick's office looking to his eyes like ripe fruit. When his mind and conversation started straying from the subject of casting she sharply reminded him that she was there to talk business. Taking this for mere banter Selznick lunged and a chase round his desk developed that Evelyn later described as 'worthy of a Marx brothers' movie'. The chase ended when Selznick ran out of puff – she was the third girl he'd seen that day – and Evelyn was able to make a semblance of a dignified exit. Selznick must have enjoyed the exercise, though, since Evelyn did, finally, play in *Gone with the Wind*. Some years later she married John Huston but always insisted they never go anywhere Selznick was likely to be.

Making a mark around town was a young actress with the looks of an angel. Selznick had long lusted after her and, with Scarlett as bait, and the girl having just been dropped by RKO, this seemed the time to make his move. He had George Cukor shoot a test then invited the girl to his office to discuss the outcome. He showed her round his various trophies and awards ending with his most prized possession, his couch. Joan Fontaine looked upon it, turned to Selznick with raised eyebrows and enquired drily, 'Scarlett?' Selznick shook his head and offered her the sister's part, Melanie. Now the word around Hollywood was that Melanie was a 'nothing' part. She would be vapid and register zero next to the vital, seething, passionate Scarlett. Joan said she wanted Scarlett or nothing. Selznick had to tell her no. On the way out the door Joan turned and waspishly said, 'Why don't you try my sister?' Joan's sister was Olivia de Havilland, a year older than Joan, and, word was, no love was lost between them. Olivia was at that time under contract to Warner's and being pursued, heavily breathing, by Howard Hughes. She had managed to make a career out of beautifully lurking while Errol Flynn fought it out in *Captain Blood*, *The Charge of the Light Brigade*, *Robin Hood* and *Dodge City*.

To escape any possible objections from Warners, Selznick had Olivia tested as Melanie on a closed set and in secret. Olivia, rated one of the world's most beautiful women, had never before had a chance at a really challenging part and saw Melanie as a way of escaping from the dreary round of vapid heroines. When Selznick saw the test he was delighted. Olivia had brought such depth and warmth to this 'nothing' part and both she and Selznick wanted her for it.

Warner's, when they heard about it, were less enthusiastic. Teamed with Flynn she was their hottest property. They didn't want her value diminished by having her cast to play a secondary role to an as yet uncast Scarlett. Olivia turned to Hughes for additional fire-power and he managed to wrench a grudging 'maybe' from Jack Warner. Now Selznick had Rhett and he had a Melanie. What about Scarlett?

Paulette Goddard was heavily promoted by Charlie Chaplin, and was tested nine times throughout 1938 but all to no avail. Paulette never forgave Selznick for the sleigh ride of expectation he put her through. Jean Arthur, an 'ex' of Selznick's, was also tested but the result was judged so awful that, by mutual consent, they burned it!

It was then that Selznick went public. He announced that after 'exhaustive' searches and tests among Hollywood's established female stars he was going to send out talent scouts to scour the entire country for a new face to play Scarlett.

This announcement sent half a million pulses racing. Girls' pulses mostly, but also some thousands of travelling salesmen's. They immediately realized that all they had to do was go into town and let drop that their real business was to look out for potential Scarletts to be besieged by girls offering whatever they wanted to get a screen test.

Very few of these swindlers were ever caught but in Flagstaff, Arizona, two of these phonies stayed one night too long and were arrested and jailed on charges of statutory rape. In Alabama they picked up no fewer than five phony Selznick scouts and prepared a long list of procuring and rape charges before being forced to drop them when the shamefaced girls refused to testify.

These arrests were hardly enough to hold back the tide. First dozens then hundreds of girls were turning up at Selznick's office clutching pieces of paper, usually scrawled on hotel notepaper, which announced them as the new Scarlett discovered by a 'chief talent scout' of whom Selznick had never heard. Most of these girls were devastated on hearing how they had been duped. Most of them were from small towns and had been 'honoured' by a send-off from the local high school band, their pictures in the local papers, and most just couldn't face going home to the humiliation of admitting they had been hoaxed. Most of them stayed on and did whatever they had to do to raise the rent and dream the dream. How many young lives were irreversibly damaged by Selznick's talent search and the tricksters who exploited it will never be known. They would have been even more devastated had they known that the whole thing was a cynical exercise to soften up America for the Scarlett which David's brother Myron had already 'found'.

Some of these young hopefuls were resourceful and provided some lighter moments. One had herself parcelled up and delivered to Selznick's office in a packing case which was labelled 'Open at once'. The harassed staff were half way through obeying this injunction when the wrappings were parted and a half-dressed girl started running wildly for Selznick's office shouting: 'Mr Selznick! Your Scarlett is here!'

Thereafter incoming mail was subjected to much more thorough scrutiny and imitators never made it past the front gate. One girl, however, managed to beat even this tighter security. She had herself delivered, on Christmas morning 1937, to Selznick's home. Selznick, surrounded by family and friends was highly embarrassed to have a naked girl spring out of the box singing: 'Happy Christmas, Mr Selznick!'

Meanwhile, out on the road, there were some genuine Selznick scouts. Oscar Serlin was looping the North Eastern States. Charles Morrison was covering the West. George Cukor travelled south with Kay Brown. In every hotel they stayed they found themselves besieged by hopeful Southern Belles. In one day, in Atlanta, they saw five hundred girls. Desperate, they wired Selznick: 'We are barricaded in our rooms. The belles have turned out in droves! Need a drink but Georgia stays a dry state!'

One girl that did make it through all Selznick's defences was a hat model called Edith Marriner. She so managed to impress Selznick that he had her tested first on 2 December 1937 and again in colour on 6 December. She didn't get the part but being tested twice was sufficient leverage to get others interested in her. Edith stayed on, changed her name to Susan Hayward, and settled into a career.

Finally Selznick tired of the charade, the 'search' having generated enough publicity to ensure the financing. Now was the time for brother Myron to come forward with the Scarlett they had had up their sleeves all along – Vivien Leigh, Myron's client.

The casting of an Englishwoman in the part of a Southern Belle created the furore that both Myron and David O had foreseen and had tried to head off with their 'search' for a new face. However, the stalling campaign had succeeded to the extent that the reigning queens of Hollywood were all so relieved that none of their close rivals had been preferred that they, nearly, all united in condemning Selznick's final choice.

The end product totally vindicated Selznick and Vivien Leigh and the finished movie was an all-time record-breaker and only inflation and increased prices of admission have displaced it from being the all-time money maker.

The less proud record of *Gone with the Wind* was Selznick's cynical nationwide publicity stunt which raised such hopes in hundreds of thousands of young girls and ruined a goodly proportion of them. Just how many of today's grandmothers secretly, possibly bitterly, remember a small town hotel room in which they dreamed of playing Scarlett O'Hara?

7

Darryl F Zanuck – Mogul of the Thirties

Darryl F Zanuck came to Hollywood in 1919. He was just seventeen years old. Short but inordinately proud of his physique and fitness, he brought with him a burning ambition to be a writer and a warped opinion of women.

The seventeen-year-old that stepped down from the train that brought him from Los Angeles had already packed more into his tender years than most men would in a lifetime. He had, at fourteen, lied about his age and joined the small and badly equipped US Army expecting to go with Pershing into Mexico to avenge the raids on the USA's territory by Pancho Villa. Instead the young Zanuck found his country declaring war on Germany and shipping him to France with the 34th Division. There he was found to be a pugnacious and courageous fly-weight boxer who soon established a reputation as unbeatable. He rose from divisional championships to become the US Army's fly-weight champion. Zanuck's prowess as a boxer kept him behind the lines and in 'training' for the short time the US was in the First World War, and so he never saw direct action. By the time he returned to the United States he was a two-year veteran of overseas wars, a boxing champion and just sixteen years old. His great mentor during his formative years had been his maternal grandfather. When Zanuck got back to his home town in Nebraska he found his grandfather ailing, and his cousins prepared to treat him like a kid. Obviously Zanuck wasn't going to stay. He left home and headed west to California where the only resident he knew was his mother.

Zanuck's mother was the cause of his life-long opinion

of women. As a young woman she had acquired a
'reputation'. Living in her father's hotels she took a liking
to the itinerants passing through and would often leave
her door open and array herself in bed with a seductive
welcoming bedside light burning. It was just such a light
which drew an unambitious clerk, Frank Zanuck, to join
her in bed one night. Grandpa thought it time to draw the
line. Frank Zanuck worked for him and sleeping with his
daughter could have only one outcome – marriage. Marriage didn't change the new Mrs Zanuck's habits one bit.
She still lived in hotels, she still left her door open at
nights. Little Darryl would often come across her in the
arms of a man she couldn't have named if her life
depended upon it. There were two things about his
mother that were to traumatize Darryl for life. One, she
had ash-blonde hair. Two, she wore, at a time when
nobody else did, bright green nail varnish. Darryl was to
have a life-long fascination with ash blondes and the
colour green. So accepted was this to become in his later
years in Hollywood that it became known as 'Zanuck
Green' and the many thousands of girls that were to cross
his casting couch wore green nail varnish as a badge of
honour.

At first, times were hard for young Zanuck, but his
eyes and ambitions were daily dazzled by the sight of
famous movie stars strolling along the boardwalk streets
of the village Hollywood as casually as 'ordinary folk'.
Zanuck was further fired by dozens of startlingly beautiful
girls who also strolled those streets. This was his kind of
town. Hollywood ignored him. He wrote magazine stories
and took odd jobs, including a spell as a professional
boxer. Then he sold a story to a pulp magazine, and then,
miraculously, through a scraped acquaintance with a star
of the time, William Russell, he sold a story to the Fox

Film Company. Other sales followed and a writing contract with Sennett followed. It was there that he met a
man who was to further reinforce his ideas about women
and their uses, Sydney Chaplin. Under Chaplin's tutelage
Zanuck came to believe that all women were whores and
that a smart man took advantage before the women 'got'
him. Chaplin told him, among other things, 'Pretty girls
are out there for the taking. They're aching for it. Give it
to them and then get out before they get their hooks into
you. There's plenty more where they came from.'

Taking Sydney Chaplin's advice Zanuck started working his way through the Sennett Bathing Beauties and, by
his word, accounted for all of them except one. The
smallest, daintiest one on the lot was a girl called Virginia
Fox. Fox was becoming a significant name to Zanuck.
He'd sold his first screenplay to the old Fox company,
now he found he was in love with a girl called Fox. He
married her, and they were to stay married for more than
fifty years.

From Sennett, Zanuck rose to writing at the Chaplin
studio but he wasn't a success. Zanuck had always thought
Chaplin a 'show-off' and a 'pompous prick'. A succession
of moves from one studio to another followed. One
afternoon Zanuck dropped into a movie house and saw
Where the North Begins a movie which featured a German
shepherd dog called Rinty. Zanuck was overwhelmed by
the bright intelligent dog that could perform tricks without
faking or cutting. He went with director Mal St Clair
directly to Warner Brothers who had made the film.
Warners were, in 1923, in trouble. They had built a
grandiose studio with all the latest facilities but hadn't
been able to make a hit. The promise held out by Zanuck
and St Clair that they could make cheap doggie pictures
found fertile ground. Warners hired them for six pictures
at $250 a week. The dog movies were a tremendous

success and the bright and intelligent Rinty had his name changed to Rin-Tin-Tin and became a Hollywood legend. Rin-Tin-Tin and Zanuck saved Warners from almost certain bankruptcy. Zanuck was pouring out screenplays as fast as his fingers could move. In 1925 he wrote more than twenty and twelve of them were big money-makers. Then Warners started to get worried that all their pictures tended to bear his name as screenwriter. To ease the situation they prevailed upon him to use pseudonyms. He had three of them and drew salaries – one for each name. Zanuck was making more money than he had ever dreamed possible. The consequences were inevitable. When Warners argued with their chief of production, Raymond Schrock, Zanuck was their natural choice as replacement.

In 1925, aged twenty-three, Zanuck took his place among the Hollywood hierarchy. He was rich, successful and, so far as anyone has been able to tell, faithful to his wife, Virginia. All that was now to change.

As a man rated high in a Hollywood rich in temptations, and still subject to the influence of Sydney Chaplin who had gone with him to Warners as a comedian, he started to stray. His first attempt in this direction ended badly. He chose reigning Warners star, Dolores Costello. Her father, a famous actor in his own right, objected to Zanuck taking 'advantage' of his daughter and talked to Virginia about it. Virginia rounded on Darryl and he withdrew from the lists for a while. His position, his own instincts and those learned first from the example of his mother, now reinforced by Chaplin, soon led to a series of daily encounters at Warners.

Meanwhile, Zanuck's star continued to rise. Warners became one of the more prosperous studios. It was about this time that Western Electric started hawking their new independent sound system around the studios. There was little interest and no takers. The movies were doing fine just as they were. Nobody wanted to upset a sure thing. Except for Harry Warner. He saw the demonstration reel and flipped for it. Everyone at Warners became enthused over the new system. The only problem was how were they going to use it. The problem landed on Zanuck's desk. It was Zanuck's wife who remembered a play about a Rabbi that they had seen in New York. At the time no one could see how to make a movie of it because so much of the plot revolved round the Rabbi's son's wish to sing 'modern' music. Zanuck saw it. Warners saw it. *The Jazz Singer* was bought and put into production. Having rejected both George Jessel and Eddie Cantor for the main role they settled for a black-face singer, Al Jolson. The picture was intended to be shot mainly in the style of the familiar silent movies with just the songs sung in synchronization with the pictures, but Jolson was an enthusiastic ad-libber, and more used to stage performance than the movies, and he would burst into a series of *spoken* ad-libs just before or after singing his songs. Warners thought Jolson was ruining these scenes with these ad-libs and wanted them cut. It was Zanuck who insisted they stay in. Not only that but Zanuck started writing in additional scenes for Jolson to *speak*. Warners pleaded with Zanuck to stop it before he ruined them. 'People might laugh when they hear that guy talk.' Zanuck was adamant and the picture went on release with synchronized dialogue sequences and all. The rest is history which owes a lot to the youthful enthusiasm of Warners' chief of production.

After *The Jazz Singer* Hollywood was never to be the same again. Warners became so rich that the Wall Street Crash hardly moved them. Zanuck was to bring further innovation when he started the famed Warners gangster series. All this adulation and fame went to Zanuck's young head. He started behaving around Warners as if he were the uncrowned king. In 1933 he realized that Warners were not going to let him join them in the highest echelons, partly because he wasn't Jewish. Jack Warner had, many years before, said: 'Darryl Francis Zanuck are three very fine gentlemen. If only one of them was Jewish I would make him a partner in the studio.'

That was Jack Warner's mistake. In 1933 Zanuck suddenly resigned Within forty-eight hours he had the finance, with Joseph Schenck, to start up their production company. Ironically their initial finance came from Louis B Mayer. Zanuck and Schenck formed Twentieth Century Films, arranging for their product to be distributed by United Artists. The films they made, despite having no home-grown stars, were financially successful largely due to Zanuck's good eye for a story. At the same time one of the oldest names in the business, Fox Films, were in trouble. They had made a series of box office failures but had two great assets – a huge studio complex with accompanying lot, and what was still the best distribution network in the business. And Zanuck was unhappy with the way United Artists were creaming off their profits. The approach to Fox was found acceptable and so the historic merger took place that created Twentieth Century-Fox. Soon Zanuck was in charge of the biggest production and distribution network in Hollywood. He was thirty-three years old.

At Warners Zanuck had been Crown Prince but as he surveyed the wide acreage that made up the Fox lot he was now nothing less than a crowned king. Along with his genius for spotting a good story came an unashamed interest in sex. His attitude to women was fairly summed up when, in a response to a rare protest from his wife Virginia, he told her, 'Why get so mad about them?

They're just tarts – girls to be fucked and thrown away. You're different. I respect you.'

Zanuck instituted a routine on the Fox lot that was to last throughout his seigneurship. Every afternoon at four o'clock a contract girl – star or starlet – would make her way through the studio to Zanuck's office. There she would be conducted into the 'secret' boudoir he had constructed behind a bookcase in his office and for precisely thirty minutes administer sexual relief to the boy wonder. These girls, rarely the same girl twice, were known as 'the four o'clock specials' and after receiving benediction from the boss could expect their contracts or their parts to undergo improvement. Many would advertise their new-found status as top girl in the Fox harem by wearing Zanuck-green nail varnish. Almost all the Fox stars passed through the 'secret' boudoir at one time or another – including Betty Grable and the most regular visitor of all, Carole Landis. It happened every afternoon and was such a part of the studio routine that movies were scheduled – in those days they scheduled them by the hour – to allow for a half-hour sex break at four in the afternoon. What was good enough for the boss was good enough for the many hundreds of writers, directors, producers and the many thousands of technicians and floor crew that would be employed on any one day. One wag suggested that the company should have a sign constructed over the studio gate which, at four in the afternoon, would change from Twentieth Century-Fox to Twentieth Century-Fucks.

Zanuck was equally uninhibited, or unrestrained, in his personal habits. The story is told of him returning one afternoon from the studio commissary when he felt an urgency in his bladder. The aides and acolytes accompanying him were surprised when, still continuing his conversation with them, he idly unbuttoned his fly and started sprinkling the flower beds. One younger aide moved discreetly to try to cover this action. Zanuck eyed the young man's move suspiciously and asked him what he was doing. The young man replied, 'Well, Sir, there're young ladies passing by and they can see you.' To which Zanuck replied, 'If you know a young lady on this lot that hasn't already seen this I want her in my office by five tonight.'

There was one female on the Fox lot who never failed to get Zanuck's attention – Shirley Temple. The little curly-haired moppet had only to cut a finger for Zanuck, personally, to rush to her side with a band aid. If anything happened to Shirley, Zanuck had to be informed immediately. Once a director called him up to tell him that Shirley had fallen and broken a tooth and moaned how this would hold up the picture. Zanuck, in conference with most of Fox's executives, replied heatedly: 'Fuck the schedule! Is Shirley in pain?' He then rushed to her side and comforted her, telling her not to worry about a thing. The picture could wait till she felt better.

Thanks to her down-to-earth parents and Zanuck's careful supervision of the biggest money maker Fox had, little Shirley grew up in the Hollywood fun factory without the slightest realization of how important she was. Her bank clerk father never quit his job, always kept a strict register of her earnings and was able to account for every cent when she came of age – unlike many less fortunate child stars who came of age to find their entire earnings soaked away in some fictional oil well or gold mine venture.

One day Shirley's unworldly father asked to see Zanuck 'urgently'. Zanuck received the man with the genuine respect he held for him. The father was troubled. He had been receiving 'certain mail' from women all over the country. Zanuck, with difficulty, extracted the information that these women were writing to him with the suggestion that he meet them and father a girl-child for them.

Zanuck asked if he could guarantee fathering them another Shirley.

'Of course not!' said the shocked Mr Temple.

'Then don't be unfaithful to your wife,' said Zanuck.

Father Temple was shocked. 'I certainly have no intention of being!' he told Zanuck.

'Then what's the problem?' asked Zanuck.

'No problem. It's just that I thought you ought to know that there are women in the world like that.'

Zanuck must have had difficulty keeping a straight face when he answered, 'That's really terrible, isn't it?'

Shirley's father started to the door, only pausing to plead with Zanuck not to tell Shirley's mother. 'She would be ashamed of her own sex,' he cautioned Zanuck.

Zanuck was at the height of his prestige and fortune when war came. Just as the fourteen-year-old had back in 1916 so did the now rich and famous Zanuck react. While most of the Hollywood Moguls simply sent for a uniform from wardrobe to walk about in, Zanuck joined up. He abandoned the good life in Hollywood and, joining the Signal Corps, set about making a series of award-winning documentaries. These were no comfortable assemblages of other people's front-line footage. Zanuck went out to North Africa, Italy, blitzed London and eventually France to shoot the material himself. His crews thought he was crazy in the way in which he insisted they get right up to, sometimes in front of, their own lines. One of them quit, saying that working for Zanuck was a sure way to get himself killed. He joined the US Marine Corps instead!

Zanuck came back from the war a very different man. He thought the war would also have changed the average American. Recognizing they would still want Betty Grable 'tit' pictures he also foresaw a market for more serious movies dealing with serious themes. He made many, for example *Gentlemen's Agreement* an attack on anti-Semitism; *Pinky*, the story of a black girl passing herself off as white; and *The Snake Pit*, an exposé of the conditions prevailing in US state mental institutions. These days such themes are commonplace in television pot-boilers but in the late forties they were pretty controversial films to make.

Fox went from strength to strength but Zanuck was getting restless presiding over a well-run, efficient production plant that was coming to be, for him, nothing more than a factory. He began to envy the European producers who could pick up one project and see it through from beginning to end. In 1955, for this among many other reasons we will investigate later, he suddenly resigned and went to Europe. Meanwhile, let us step back to the beginning of the forties.

8

The Forties – War and Witch-hunts

During the thirties Hollywood had enjoyed an almost uninterrupted prosperity. At the beginning of the decade talking pictures were a novelty; by the end the medium had been mastered and the industry entered the forties making pictures of real merit that were dominating the world markets. Only a catastrophe could prevent Hollywood's dreams from becoming the world's dreams. That catastrophe duly appeared in the shape of the Second World War.

Overnight the immensely valuable European market disappeared. Although America didn't enter the war until late 1941 the majority of Americans sympathized with the anti-Nazi struggle and Hollywood quickly reflected this. The rise of Nazism and the growing inevitability of war in Europe had been largely ignored by the Hollywood dream factory, but when real war started Hollywood pulled out all the stops. First a trickle, then a stream and finally a flood of war films were made. Most of them were simple-minded patriotic hymns but others were reworkings of old plots with a new war slant. Also much in demand was escapist entertainment, and so began the rise of the pin-up glamour girl. Hollywood was to discover a new Klondike. Audiences seemed to be prepared to lay siege to any theatre no matter what was showing and profits soared as never before.

These boom years were to be somewhat marred by the departure of so many established male stars into genuine war service. Jimmy Stewart, Clark Gable, Robert Taylor, Robert Montgomery, Victor Mature, Tyrone Power,

Henry Fonda, Mickey Rooney and many others joined the rush to get into the forces and see action. Many other stars, considered unfit for military service, went off instead on morale-raising tours of army bases taking with them many of the female stars.

Of all the stars who went to war, and saw genuine front-line action, only one died on what might be called active service and that was Carole Lombard, wife of Clark Gable. She died in a plane crash in Nevada while returning from a War Bond rally.

Most of the Moguls, apart from Darryl Zanuck, confined themselves to wearing their wardrobe uniforms to their studios. Harry Cohn, Tsar of Columbia, made his anti-fascist gesture by removing the signed photograph of Mussolini from his office wall. Cohn had come to admire Mussolini when his reputation had been based on getting the Italian trains to run on time – quite a feat for a service that thought nothing of trains being a *day* or two late! Cohn had been much impressed by Il Duce's office with its long intimidating walk to the desk, which was on a raised dais with the sun blinding the visitor as it came through the windows directly behind the Italian dictator. Harry Cohn had his own office modelled on similar lines. He didn't bother redecorating when war broke out.

The outbreak of war in Europe was to have profound effects on the careers of two actresses in particular. Much has been written about the 'mystery' of Greta Garbo's sudden retirement from films 'at the height of her career'. There was no mystery. Garbo's films had never really registered with the American public but had been strong earners in the European markets where a Garbo picture could be used to lever a reluctant European distributor into taking a great deal of weaker product in a package. That alone justified her contract price while the earnings from her movies in Europe put them, also, into profit.

With Europe in flames that market was destroyed and with it went the logic of keeping an expensive loss-leader like Garbo. She didn't appeal in the US market because she did so little in her parts. She was often referred to as a blank canvas on which the audience could superimpose their own emotions. US audiences went to the movies to be entertained by others' creativity, not to exercise their own. Looking back over Garbo's films they appear to be simply the same picture over and over again. Garbo invested all her roles with great placid beauty and all the emotional fire of a speak-your-weight machine. Her contract no longer made sense without the European market and so she was, gently, dropped.

The other part of the legend that Garbo had tired of Hollywood and preferred anonymity is also nonsense. Throughout the forties she desperately tried to get another chance but no one was prepared to take the risk. By the time the war ended and the European market was re-established Garbo was a faded memory. Tastes had changed. Garbo smouldering indolently for ninety minutes was not going to hold audiences conditioned to expect action.

Marlene Dietrich, she of the sewing circle, had experienced similar difficulties during the late thirties but her redeeming feature, and the one that was to see her through a lustrous career, was a sense of humour and self-parody, something Garbo never had. Garbo saw herself as nothing less than a great actress to whom simple worship was due, and when rejection came she couldn't take it.

Garbo's replacement was already in Hollywood – Ingrid Bergman. She made her first film in 1939 on the very eve of the outbreak of war in Europe. *Intermezzo*, with Leslie Howard, was a remake of her original Swedish hit. American audiences took to her immediately, finding in her a freshness and naturalness that had been absent from the more aloof Garbo. For all her sweet naturalness there was a burning ambition inside Ingrid which might be one of the reasons she was always blinded to the reality of the world around her. She came to Hollywood immediately after making a film in Germany, which she saw as the true home of creative film making. Hollywood was for money, Germany for artistic triumph.

Her contract with David O Selznick was unique in two respects. Firstly it stipulated that *she* had an option of getting out if her first film was not a success. Secondly, and concealed from the public at the time, was that she refused to appear in any film that was detrimental to Germany or the Nazis. This was less a political stance than a safeguard against her 'true' artistic home. Ingrid was half-German and within the German half of her family the usual greeting was 'Heil Hitler'. With war already declared Ingrid returned to her native Sweden to make *Juninatten*, still believing that she would be able, as a neutral, to make films in both Germany and the United States. Although strongly tempted by an offer from Berlin she did in fact return to the United States where she played on the New York stage in *Lilom*.

Having arrived in Hollywood as a star Ingrid had no need of the usual horizontal ladder to success, but she used sex, reportedly in a passionless objective way, in order to establish ascendancy over whichever director and co-star she happened to be working with. It was just one more tool to be deployed in the main objective of making Ingrid Bergman a bigger star. While this ploy seemed to work superbly well during her time in Hollywood, it came slightly awry when she came across a passionate Italian, in the shape of Roberto Rossellini, who had recently directed the impressive *Open City*. Ingrid wrote to him out of the blue, asking if he had any use for a Swedish actress. Ingrid was a world star at the time and Rossellini was struggling to find finance. Ingrid was a godsend to him and he wrote back, probably inspired by the two words of Italian she had included in her note, which Rossellini translated as 'I love you'. They joined forces to make *Stromboli* and a baby.

Unfortunately for Ingrid this was her first false move. American mothers' groups were outraged that 'their' Swede should give birth to another man's child while still married to her husband, Swedish businessman Per Lindstrom. Ingrid was perplexed by this furore. For her there was a distinct difference between her personal life and her professional life. Professionally, however, Rossellini turned out to be a dud. They made three more pictures, each worse than the previous one, until they lurched on the edge of bankruptcy. Ingrid split the passionate relationship the moment she was offered *Anastasia* by Twentieth Century-Fox. Ingrid ended her seven-year-long exile, imposed by various moral pressure groups, and started to pick up the threads of her international career. Her first three 'rehabilitating' films – the other two were *The Inn of the Sixth Happiness* and *Indiscreet* – were all made in England but after that offers started getting fewer. She made a film in France, where she was now living, and that was really the end of Bergman as an international screen star. There was television and some success on stage still to come but all that determined ambition had been burned out in the one passionate affair she had ever allowed herself. Maybe Ingrid's instinct had been right in the first place. Keep emotion on the screen and sex strictly for business.

Meanwhile, back in Hollywood proper, nothing was changing. The wartime years were to be the years of the shakedown artist. Among the many thousands of young hopefuls who turned up yearly in Hollywood came, in 1940, a pretty enough sixteen-year-old from Minnesota, Sylvia Platt. Sylvia had come more in hope than anything else. Knowing nobody she was ripe for the many leeches that were ready to hang themselves onto anyone as wide-eyed as she was.

Sylvia found her leech in the shape of one Virginia Lopez. Dazzling Sylvia with her interest and her apparent access to the homes of the famous, Virginia moved Sylvia into her own home and started tutoring her in how things were done in Hollywood. Sylvia had never heard of such behaviour back home and, at first, baulked at the suggestion that she 'play ball' with the rich and famous. What she didn't know was that Virginia was a well known purveyor of young flesh to some of the wilder Hollywood party people. Among these Lionel Atwill, an actor who had made sinister villain parts all his own throughout the thirties. Virginia brought Sylvia along to Atwill's New Year's Eve party of 1940, as part of a job lot of near virgins.

Atwill, along with his Philadelphia socialite wife – ex-wife of General Douglas MacArthur, shortly to find himself busy in the Philippines – enjoyed the more exotic forms of sexual diversion, into which Sylvia was duly plunged. Sylvia, whose previous experience hadn't extended beyond back-seat necking with high school boys, constantly sought confirmation from Virginia that she was doing the right thing. Reassured, Sylvia seems to have started enjoying herself – after all there were some famous names there she had previously only seen on the screen or heard about. Heady stuff for an innocent Minnesotan girl.

Several weeks into the New Year Sylvia noticed something missing from her monthly routine and took her worry to Lopez. Neither had a hope of identifying who, among the many, might be the father and, to Lopez, this was an irrelevance anyway. She struck straight at the centre – Atwill. Atwill, concerned, reacted as any gentleman would, and started calling round his fellow guests at his New Year's bash calling for contributions for a fund to 'save ourselves a whole lot of bother'. All those contacted saw the sense of doing the decent thing and the contributions started rolling in. Lopez waited, sure she was onto another big score. Unfortunately she had overlooked one thing, letting Sylvia in on the shakedown angle – probably because she had intended keeping the lion's share, after medical expenses, for herself.

Sylvia, scared, called home and asked for the money to take care of the problem. Mom and Dad reacted by calling the local police who went through to their Beverly Hills counterparts and enquiries were set in motion. Sylvia told all before Lopez could stop her and Atwill faced charges of statutory rape brought by Sylvia's indignant parents who had hurried to their daughter's side. Lopez tried frantically to get them to drop the charges since it was obvious that she wasn't going to collect if matters got into open court.

Atwill, his career at stake, went into the witness box and deploying all his suave charm convinced the judge that he had conducted nothing more outrageous than an inspirational prayer meeting. The 'blue' films referred to by the complainants were, he told the court, nothing but travelogues and religious films. The clinching argument came when Atwill declared: 'Nothing of the kind suggested could possibly have occurred. My wife was present throughout!' That was enough for the judge, who couldn't imagine that a 'wife' could possibly have enjoyed such shenanigans herself. All charges were dismissed. Half a hundred Hollywood names breathed easily for the first time in months.

Matters might have rested there except for an unfortunate misunderstanding over some bouncing cheques which placed one of Atwill's chief defence witnesses behind bars. The aggrieved convicted man felt that Atwill owed him for his perjured testimony in court and was mad as hell at being in jail when a few thousand dollars from Atwill, for which he had never asked, could have saved him. He contacted the Los Angeles District Attorney and offered, in exchange for a reduced sentence, to reconsider his evidence in support of Atwill. Atwill was rearrested and charged on two counts of giving perjured evidence. Atwill again gave a polished performance in court, admitting some of the charges, and claiming that he lied 'like a gentleman' to protect his friends. He also told the judge, justifiably, that he was the victim of a shakedown which had gone wrong. The judge was once again impressed and handed down a light probation order when he could have given a heavy jail sentence. Atwill was free, but not out of the woods. The Hays Code stipulated that no one on probation could be employed in the movies and Atwill's contract was ended. It was obscurity for Atwill, who never again climbed back on the golden bandwagon.

Of little Sylvia and her offspring we know nothing. She was as much a victim of Lopez as was Atwill. Knowing nothing of the plot to get money she had done what any other scared kid would have done and called her mother. With a little less greed from Lopez, or a little more honesty towards Sylvia, the world would have kept turning and, maybe, both she and Atwill would have continued their careers.

The next shakedown was aimed at Errol Flynn and this time came from an interesting source – the Los Angeles police headquarters. They had picked up a girl called Betty Hansen on vagrancy and prostitution charges. Frightened, the girl offered to tell 'all' about the time she had been to a swimming party with Errol Flynn and Bruce Cabot. The cops were interested because they hadn't been getting their share of the huge wartime profits being made by Flynn's studio – Warners. Regular contributions were expected from all the major studios in return for which the cops ignored minor infringements and discouraged others from laying potentially embarrassing charges. Warners hadn't, in the police department's opinion, been coming up with enough, and Betty Hansen seemed a good vehicle by which to render a reminding tug on the chain.

Flynn was arrested and charged with statutory rape. After Flynn returned home from being booked an unidentified male voice called up on his phone and said, 'Tell Jack I want $100,000,' and hung up.

Flynn immediately informed Jack Warner who tried to find out where the mystery call had come from. Warner's own enquiries turned up the information that Betty Hansen and another girl, Margaret Satterlee, also about to give evidence against Flynn, had both originally been arrested on prostitution charges. After hearing Flynn's side of the story Warners decided to fight. They hired Jerry Geisler who, in court, proceeded to tear both girls' evidence to shreds, establishing to everyone's satisfaction that both girls had been more than willing and that they had been well paid. The most telling fact against the Hansen girl's evidence was that there had been a full year's gap between the alleged offence and her deciding that she wanted to complain. Since there was no doubt in anybody's mind that Flynn could, and did, have any girl he wanted without coercion, the charges were dismissed.

How many girls had given their 'all' on the casting couch will never be known. Unique on the distaff side was director Ernst Lubitsch. He died on it.

Lubitsch had come from Germany to Hollywood in the

twenties, and rapidly established a reputation as a director of stylish comedies. His other, less public, reputation was as an enthusiastic user of the casting couch. Lubitsch always insisted on a two-week rehearsal period before starting a picture. During this period of creative exploration, Lubitsch would lock himself away with his leading ladies and find ways of adding to his on-screen reputation as the man who could make sex funny.

In 1935 Lubitsch found himself promoted to production chief at Paramount. He felt himself ill-suited for the executive role and, at the same time, the target for many a cruel hoax, which did nothing for his heart condition. Scheduled to appear at the opening of *Belle of the Nineties* in San Francisco, he found that he could only fit it into his schedule if he overcame his well-known fear of flying. It was with difficulty that he was persuaded that flying was the only solution.

Clinging desperately to his seat, Lubitsch was taken aloft in a twin-engined charter plane. His worst fears about flying seemed realized when, over Santa Barbara, the plane began to buck wildly, seemingly out of control. Lubitsch started screaming forward to the two pilots to 'do something'. The two men appeared from the cockpit wearing, Lubitsch saw, parachutes! 'We don't know what you're going to do,' they told him, 'but we're getting the hell out!' Paralyzed with fear, Lubitsch watched as the two 'pilots' swung open the door and leapt out into the night!

Lubitsch collapsed to the floor of the aircraft with a heart seizure, and was little comforted to learn later that the two men that had parachuted out were not the pilots but two stunt men hired to put the fear of God into him. There is no record of how well Lubitsch enjoyed *Belle of the Nineties*, the picture he had been on his way to see.

Lubitsch gave up his executive duties shortly thereafter and returned to directing, but somehow the old magic had left him. The two pictures he made under the remainder of his Paramount contract were not successful and he left Paramount to work at MGM. There he started a writing association with the rising Billy Wilder who did much of the dialogue on *Ninotchka*. The success of the picture depended more on Billy Wilder's writing than on Lubitsch's direction.

In 1941 Wilder was on his way to see Lubitsch for discussions on their next joint project. Arriving at Lubitsch's office he heard some faint calls of distress from a girl. Wilder hesitated. Lubitsch's habit of taking a little sexual relaxation with some passing starlet was well known and he didn't want to intrude. He listened for a while and heard what he thought were cries from the girl of increasing distress. Pushing open the door Wilder found an hysterical blonde pinned to the couch by the considerable weight of Lubitsch. 'He's dead!' screamed the blonde. Wilder carefully eased Lubitsch from the hysterical girl, calmed her down, gave her the cab fare home and set about tidying the place up before calling an ambulance. Lubitsch, the man who made sex funny, had given his life for it.

There is a postscript to this story which clearly delineates the prevailing attitudes in Hollywood. The morning after Lubitsch's tragic death, and before it was made public, another blonde hopeful turned up in Lubitsch's office. She had an appointment with him. As gently as they could, secretaries told her that Lubitsch was no longer able to keep the appointment since he had died. The young lady was shocked and disappointed. 'But he promised me a part in his picture!' she blubbered. Again the secretaries told her that Lubitsch was unable to keep his promise through no fault of his own. Bitterly disappointed the young lady turned to leave. At the door she turned back for one last despairing try. 'Did he leave any messages?' she asked.

Paulette Goddard came to Hollywood by the well trodden road of a Ziegfeld Follies chorus girl. Observing all the conventions that being a fourteen-year-old Ziegfeld girl implied she was soon taken up by the usual stage door roués. At sixteen she managed to separate one from the herd – a millionaire who had his fortune in the lumber business – and married him. The marriage lasted three years, after which Miss Goddard collected a tidy half-million-dollar settlement and, aged nineteen, set out to conquer Hollywood. Her capital ensured she moved in the best Hollywood circles even though she only got walk-ons and bit parts. Hal Roach was impressed enough to give her a contract and a reputation as a fun girl to have at a party. It was in the party spirit that she was invited aboard Joe Schenck's yacht for a weekend cruise. Also aboard was the now forty-six-year-old Charlie Chaplin. Miss Goddard might have seemed a little too mature for his eye, but their first weekend upon the high seas was later described as 'hot stuff'. Chaplin was certainly smitten since he bought her contract from Hal Roach and set about grooming Paulette for her first co-starring role in the film he was then planning, *Modern Times*. In all things Chaplin was meticulous but the four years it took to bring *Modern Times* before the cameras was excessive even for him. Even more so when it is remembered that it was shot as a silent movie eight years after everyone else had started making sound films. It was also highly derivative of a French movie, *A Nous La Liberté*, made many years before it. Everyone predicted a dismal failure for *Modern Times*, but once again the Chaplin genius outwitted them. It was the second highest grossing picture of its year.

Meanwhile jealous Charlie kept Paulette all to himself until he made strenuous efforts to get her the Scarlett

O'Hara role in *Gone with the Wind*. When even Chaplin couldn't get her the part Paulette decided he was hindering rather than helping. She broke away from him to make *The Ghost Breakers* in 1940 and then accepted a small part of a gypsy girl in Cecil B de Mille's *North West Mounted Police*. It was Paulette's bizarre social life that nearly ruined the sneak preview of *North West Mounted Police*.

On the very day of the preview scurrilous rumours started circulating Hollywood. It seemed that the previous night Paulette and her dinner companion had been overcome with amorous intentions and Paulette had slipped to her knees and started vigorously administering sexual gratification in full view of the other diners in Ciro's, a well known restaurant. The story went that the waiters had been forced to form a screen round the amorous pair when the entreaties of the head waiter had failed to dissuade Miss Goddard from carrying matters to a head.

Cecil B de Mille, knowing nothing of these rumours, was somewhat disconcerted when the students from nearby UCLA started barracking the movie, and in particular Paulette's lines. When she told Robert Preston, on screen, 'I think I eat your heart out!' the delighted collegiate audience yelled back: 'Didn't you get enough last night?'

Worse was to come. Her next line was, 'I'd come to you even if you were on the other side of the moon!' To which the audience yelled, 'Try Ciro's! It's closer!'

De Mille was on his feet, now bewildered as to why his lines were attracting so much derision. When Robert Preston, as the Mountie, tells Paulette, 'You little wildcat! Nobody could ever make me let you go!' someone yelled: 'Not even the head waiter!' and the preview dissolved into farce as not one further word of dialogue could be heard.

De Mille left the theatre furiously demanding to know why his film had been made into a fiasco. Someone told him the stories that were going around and he swore never to speak to Miss Goddard ever again. Something must have changed his mind because he did use her in *The Unconquered* which one critic called *The Unspeakable*.

Paulette survived all the derision and went on to become one of Paramount's top stars in a career that was to last until the late sixties.

What of her ex-lover Charlie Chaplin? Having figured in a scandal in each of our decades we surely can't leave him out of the forties. No, Charlie will not disappoint us. In 1941 when he was fifty-two a young starlet, Joan Barry, came to his studio for an audition. She had found her way there during a 'party girl' chore where she had met, and influenced, a talent scout who knew talent when it got into his bed. 'Sure-fire' was the introduction Joan got to Chaplin, who might have noticed some resemblance to Paulette Goddard. Whatever happened during that first interview it fired Charlie with enthusiasm. He announced that he had discovered a new 'star' and that she would be 'groomed' for a forthcoming picture. Joan got a contract at $100 a week and expenses for her abortions (two in her first year). Her grooming for the screen was less successful and as their relationship declined Charlie cut her contractual salary to $25 a week. No one ever accused Chaplin of being generous. He seems to have been surprised when Joan took exception to her ejection from his house and the salary cut. She took to harassing him at home. One Sunday afternoon Charlie was chatting with some guests when one of them drew his attention to the fact that there was a naked girl on his lawn dancing in and out of the sprinklers. Charlie saw none other than Joan Barry. He turned off the water and shouted at her to go away. Joan answered by aiming bricks through his windows. Chaplin called the cops who, after hearing Joan's side of the story, returned and advised Chaplin that he would be doing everyone a favour if he paid Miss Barry's expenses back to New York from whence she had come. Charlie accepted the cops' advice – an act which was to have disastrously expensive consequences for him.

In May 1943 Miss Barry came back, this time brandishing a gun and threatening to kill either herself, him or both. Chaplin calmed her down, took her inside and, according to Miss Barry, proceeded to make love to her three times almost without stopping. He then gave her more money and urged her to return to New York and to 'stop being silly'. At that time it was Chaplin's intention to marry the seventeen-year-old daughter of playwright Eugene O'Neill, though this was not yet public knowledge. Obviously Joan Barry could have been an embarrassment at such a moving time in his life. Joan said she would go quietly, but on the way to Pasadena she heard about Chaplin's coming marriage and, turning round, went right back and broke into his house while he was out, took off her clothes and got into bed. Chaplin was furious when he found her – no love-making this time. Instead he called the cops, who were rapidly tiring of the charade. They took Joan away, charged her with housebreaking, and the judge sent her to jail for thirty days.

Just as Miss Barry was being set free Charlie, now fifty-five, married seventeen-year-old Oona O'Neill. Joan had, during her stay as a guest of California State, discovered that she was pregnant and slapped a suit on the smiling groom. That might have been enough to spoil any seventeen-year-old's honeymoon, but worse was to come. Because Chaplin had paid Joan Barry's fare to New York and she had used money he had given her to buy her ticket back, he was charged under the Mann Act with transporting a girl across State lines for immoral purposes! The fact that he had given her the money on the advice of two Beverly Hills cops was considered irrelevant. So too was the fact that the money he had given her was for her to stay away – not come back! Charlie was indicted. On the paternity suit Charlie denied being the father but nevertheless made a lump sum payment and agreed to a $100-a-week maintenance until after the birth of the baby when, he was confident, blood tests would bear him out. The baby was born and the blood tests *did* show that Chaplin was not the father. Nevertheless, Chaplin was ordered to pay Joan Barry maintenance. The Mann Act charges were quietly dropped but the press was on Charlie's tail. He was accused of getting rich in the US while refusing to become a US citizen. He was further inferred to be a communist. He and Oona threw in the towel and, when the war ended, left the States to settle in Switzerland.

During the paternity suit hearing Chaplin had been asked questions about his potency. Chaplin told them he was quite virile, thank you, and then, with Oona, proceeded to prove it by fathering eight children – the last when he was into his seventies! Obviously Oona had found the secret of keeping Charlie and scandal away from each other!

Rita Hayworth was born Margarita Carmen Cansino, the daughter of Eduardo Cansino, who was a fiercely protective father. He schooled his daughter to become his own partner and Margarita debuted at a swish Mexican border night club much frequented by the Hollywood corps out on a spree. Eduardo hoped that this showcase would get him elevated to the movies but it was Margarita that caught the roving eye of Winfield Sheehan, head of production at Fox. Sheehan signed her at the age of sixteen, to a contract which paid her, at her father's insistence, $200 a week. She played mostly Spanish or Mexican dancers until Sheehan planned her first real leading role in *Ramona* which, at seventeen, would have been a big breakthrough for her. Unfortunately this was the time that Darryl F Zanuck's Twentieth Century Films took over the Fox lot. First casualty was Winfield Sheehan, second was Margarita's chance to star in *Ramona*. Zanuck had looked at the tests and not been much impressed by the raven-haired Spanish-looking girl. He called her into his office to 'assess' her. Margarita, he found, was the only virgin on the lot apart from Shirley Temple, and determined to stay that way. Zanuck terminated her contract and replaced her with the much more accessible Loretta Young.

Margarita's hopes were crushed. She returned to the protective arms of her father and told him the real reason she hadn't got the part. Eduardo consoled his daughter by telling her that virtue was more important than movie stardom. Something clicked in the mind of Margarita who, until that time, had believed that all wisdom and good advice emanated solely from her father.

A year later she had her very first date with a man – balding forty-year-old Edward Judson. Judson, a car salesman, saw something vital in young Margarita – a ticket to riches for himself. He assiduously wooed the young girl, who knew practically nothing about men and was totally flattered, first by his attentions and then by his absolute faith that she could be a star. She married Judson on 29 May 1937 to the intense displeasure of her father, who was about the same age as the groom. Judson, true to his word, started working on his wife's career. Margarita was entranced. Here was a man who seemed as wise as her father had been, more convinced of her talent and shared her burning ambitions. Also he had introduced her to the previously unsuspected delights of sex.

Judson was a man with a purpose: to make Margarita a star. He took her along to Columbia where he secured her a contract at $250 a week. There she played in a series of B-pictures, changed her name, first to Rita Cansino and then, adapting her mother's maiden name of Hatworth, to Rita Hayworth. Her mother was a sister to Ginger Rogers' mother, making Rita and Ginger cousins. Ginger was the reigning star of the RKO lot and Judson took a close look to see what the difference between them was. He decided it was the hair. He got Columbia's hairdressing department to come up with a reddish blonde tint and to submit Rita to a series of painful depilation treatments that raised her hair-line. Rita was transformed from a raven-haired Spanish type to a cool long-legged Anglo-Saxon. Judson then started pushing her at Harry Cohn. Cohn proved more receptive to her personally, and Rita was startled that Judson apparently condoned her visits to the Cohn couch. Still Cohn wasn't sure about her screen persona. Cohn had never before created a star, relying on loan-outs from other studios. He couldn't see one when she was under his nose. Instead he was surprised at the amount of interest being shown by other studios – RKO and Warners. It was on these loan-outs that Rita became a star in *Strawberry Blonde* and *Affectionately Yours*. Somewhat belatedly Zanuck saw Rita in a new light and, having trouble with Carole Landis, he took her out of *Blood and Sand* and replaced her with a now much more willing Rita Hayworth. Cohn, who owned her contract still, was amazed at the rapid rise of his B-movie actress. He started taking an interest in her career and moved her into the notorious number one dressing room which had direct access, via a secret door, to his office. With both Cohn and Zanuck taking an 'interest' and her husband happily colluding, Rita's career soared. Columbia was to hit real pay dirt when they teamed her with Glenn Ford for *Gilda* in 1946. In 1943 Rita startled everybody when she divorced Judson after he started making trouble after finding her in bed with co-star Victor Mature. Judson wanted $30,000 severance money which Rita refused to pay. Judson threatened to tell all about her rise to stardom via the couches of the Moguls, to which he had introduced and schooled her. Rita told him to go ahead. Cohn, however, thought $30,000 was cheap at the price and paid it himself.

That same year Rita met and married Hollywood wunderkind Orson Welles. Welles had astounded the public with his *Citizen Kane* and now he astonished them by marrying the reigning sex goddess. Cohn groaned. He'd had nothing but trouble from Judson and expected even more from Welles. He was astonished when it didn't come. Welles was far more interested in his own projects than anything Rita might be doing. In Welles Rita had again found a man she could listen to. Having decided that her mind could do with some improving he set her a course of books to read, which Rita did with great enthusiasm. Meanwhile she seemed to have become more pliant than ever. She shot *Tonight and Every Night* while pregnant with her first baby, Rebecca Welles, who was born within weeks of the movie's completion. A few weeks after the birth she was back at work rehearsing her dance numbers for *Gilda*. It was after *Gilda* that the trouble Cohn had first feared started to materialize. Rita's reading, plus her elevation to undoubted first-rank stardom made her much more choosy about the scripts she was offered. She either turned them down or used delaying tactics when she was forced into something she didn't want to do. These problems were less to do with Welles than with the deterioration in their marriage. Welles was spending more and more time away from her and finally, in 1948, they officially separated.

Seeking solace among 'true' friends, Rita went to spend a weekend with the Zanucks – Virginia and Darryl – at their Palm Springs home. Rita arrived shortly after lunch to be greeted by Virginia Zanuck. Rita barely drew breath before being introduced to a short, dark, superbly handsome man, Prince Aly Khan. Their eyes locked and both seemed to be ignoring the introductions and hostessy fussing of Virginia Zanuck. Suddenly, to the surprise of all present, and barely having exchanged a word, they left the room hand in hand and headed for Aly's weekend bedroom where they proceeded to stay for most of their visit.

This was bad news for Aly's current movie star 'fiancée', Gene Tierney. She had spent many a weekend with Aly at the Zanucks' and nursed hopes of marrying him when his promised divorce came through. Aly ducked the confrontation and after his passionate weekend with Rita headed for Europe. Rita soon enraged Columbia by following him, saying she needed 'a rest'. She travelled to Paris, her first ever visit to Europe, with her secretary as sole companion. There she found that things were different. Aly was out on the town with a different girl every night and not the slightest bit flattered or fazed when love-lorn Rita turned up. She was old news and he couldn't understand what more she expected.

Rita retaliated by setting out, disguised in a dark wig and heavy glasses, to have a debauch of her own. Every roué in Paris in the late forties has a 'Rita' story and most of them are fiction. One story, true or not, is probably worth repeating. It seems that one lucky Pierre spent an evening whispering into her ear with the result that she agreed to fit him in the following night. Pierre, with a reputation as an expert seducer of women to protect, prepared both himself and his apartment meticulously –

champagne, low lights and mood-making music. His Hollywood quarry arrived nearly two hours late, cast one look around the apartment and asked for the bathroom. Delighted to see her, he bowed her towards the requested facility. Five minutes later Rita emerged stark naked and asked for directions to the bedroom. Pierre protested: 'The champagne . . . the dinner, first we must . . .' Rita waved all this aside. 'I haven't time for that crap. You want to fuck or don't you?' Pierre couldn't. He was desolated and impotent for a month afterwards.

Rita emerged from her Parisian odyssey when she heard from Elsa Maxwell, then resident in Cannes, that Aly was in Cannes and spoke of nobody but her. The grand reunion took place at Elsa's house and from that night onward Aly and Rita were inseparable as they travelled and scandalized the world together. Each was, at that moment, still married to someone else.

Harry Cohn was furious. The only star that Columbia had ever created was busily wrecking, he thought, her value. On 27 May 1949 the critics of their flagrant, passion-filled affair were somewhat quieted when they married. Two years and a daughter later, they were divorced. Rita returned to work out her contract with Columbia. Cohn rushed her into *Salome* and *Sadie Thompson*, but something was missing. She never regained the popularity she had enjoyed before Aly. After more fights with Cohn he sadly came to a momentous decision: 'Screw her!' he told his minions. 'We'll make a new star!'

One slightly plaintive footnote to Rita's story is a remark she once made. 'The trouble with me and men is that they go to bed with Gilda and wake up with me . . .'

Gene Tierney came to Hollywood via some good parts on Broadway. She was first drawn to MGM where she tested for *National Velvet* when she was seventeen. The movie was temporarily postponed and Gene called up an acquaintance, director Anatole Litvak, who had a year previously been much struck with the sloe-eyed beautiful teenager. Litvak had then urged her to try her luck in Hollywood but her parents, rightly suspecting Litvak's true intentions towards their cherished daughter, talked her out of it. Instead young Gene took drama lessons and got some quite good parts on Broadway, which led MGM to offer her the test. Litvak was delighted to hear from her though somewhat inhibited by being newly married to Miriam Hopkins. He introduced her to his old friend and confidant, Darryl Zanuck. Zanuck was much struck by the beautiful teenager and fitted her into his four o'clock timetable with consummate ease. It so happened that Gene could act and Zanuck, much impressed, put her directly into a starring role in *The Return of Frank James* opposite Henry Fonda, directed by Fritz Lang. The following year she was directed by John Ford in *Tobacco Road*, Henry Hathaway in *Sundown*, and Irving Cummings in *Belle Starr*. An impressive start for any actress. Twentieth Century had discovered a major star. Marriage to Oleg Cassini, Hollywood's leading dress designer, was followed by the birth of a retarded child. Gene blamed herself for the child's condition – she had German measles during the pregnancy. It was to start a twenty-year slide, not helped by broken affairs with Tyrone Power, Aly Khan and pursuit by Howard Hughes. To this was added the ongoing afternoon appointments with Zanuck. Alcohol proved no easy means of blocking out the pressure and attempted comebacks ended in prolonged psychiatric treatments. Her fall from stardom, even though Zanuck proved a loving and loyal friend, was not helped when her parents divorced and her father sued *her* for maintenance!

Howard Hughes was an original. Aviation, the movies, psychiatry, Hughes contributed in one way or another to the annals of them all. Both his parents were dead by the time he was eighteen in 1923, and he went to court to have himself declared legally adult so he could be in charge of his own affairs. He took control of his father's machine-tool business, and immediately bought out the remaining shareholders and took off, with his millions, for Hollywood.

Standing six foot four, appearing shy, deferential, this young multi-millionaire with a declared interest in making movies attracted the excited attentions of Hollywood women. Initially the male-dominated establishment thought him a soft touch and prepared to catch the naïve Texan, and his millions, in their varied velvet traps. Hughes soon showed them he was going to be as independent in movie-making as in all other things. He truly believed that when you contracted an actress you literally owned her. Now, this was the de facto philosophy prevailing at the time with the Moguls exerting, or seeking to exert, total control over their contracted talent and, with the girls at least, *droit de seigneur* over their bodies. Hughes took all this on literally.

He had come to Hollywood in 1926 with an equally young wife, Ella Rice, but considered his marriage merely an inconvenience as he succumbed to the waves of women that found him attractive. His first Hollywood conquest, although no one can be certain, is said to have been Billie Dove. Ex-Ziegfeld, ex-Mack Sennett Bathing Beauty, Billie had risen to become one of Hollywood's most valuable stars. Hughes met her at the premiere of *The Black Pirate*, one of the first two-colour Technicolor movies made, and whisked the beauteous and willing twenty-six-year-old star to an immediate bedding. This early success with one of the biggest current names in Hollywood released a pent-up passion which he had never previously suspected existed. Howard Hughes, just twenty-one years old, found himself in a veritable candy store of available women. Over-supplied with 'pocket money' the kid set about buying up the store. Jean Harlow, contracted and therefore 'owned', was a routine bed-mate and the youthful Hughes wanted the excitement of the chase. Katharine Hepburn became an early target. He chased her across the country, piloting his own plane, until she terminated what she later described as a 'boring romance'. Ginger Rogers was another conquest who walked when she found him in bed with Jean Harlow. Hughes' movie making continued apace after the huge success of *Hell's Angels*. None matched it until first *The Front Page* and then *Scarface* (1932) which became a *cause célèbre* between himself and the Hays Office who wanted heavy cuts. Hughes fought them all the way, kept most of what he wanted, and saw the picture go out to be a smash hit. About this time he grew bored with the movie business and, much to the relief of the Hollywood Moguls, aviation became his first love. He founded the Hughes Aircraft Company and started acquiring an airline, TWA. His interest in Hollywood's women, however, did not diminish. He is rumoured to have bedded most and propositioned dozens of others. The list of notables is almost too long to list – just check the relevant casting directories – but Hughes found the whole business of pursuit too lengthy and too time consuming. Like any well-trained executive he learned to delegate. He started a detective agency with the sole brief to track down any girl that took his fancy, whether by way of a movie appearance or her picture in a newspaper or magazine. These girls, when traced, were extensively grilled and, if willing, offered a personal contract with Hughes. Now, attentive readers will remember that Hughes regarded a contract as a full title to every aspect of a girl's life. Nobody will ever know for certain but it is estimated that Hughes was supporting anything from fifty to a hundred girls at any one time. Each girl would be given an apartment or hotel room, a weekly income and told to stay put until sent for. Hughes kept a filing system with him at all times, complete with names and addresses, descriptions and whatever was known of the girl's background. Most of these girls never got to meet Hughes, let alone get to Hollywood or start their promised careers. Those that did will never forget the encounter. One such lady describes how she was roused from sleep by a persistent knocking and ringing of her doorbell. Hastily donning a dressing gown she enquired through the door who it was that had woken her. 'Howard Hughes,' came the reply. She opened the door to find him practically filling the door frame. She had been under contract to Hughes for nearly ten months but had never seen or spoken to him before. 'He grunted when I opened the door, and pushed past me into the apartment carrying a small suitcase. While I still stood staring at the legend to whom I was contracted, he sat himself down and started kicking off his shoes. He had yet to look at me. When I asked him if he wanted a drink or something, he barely shook his head before standing and asking where the bathroom was. I pointed it out to him and his absence gave me a moment to think. I had never met this man. He hadn't even looked at me. His shoes lay, threateningly, on the carpet. For the past months I had been "kept" by him, cheques coming as regular as clockwork from the Hughes Tool Company. Now here he was at well past midnight in "our" apartment and here, it seemed, for the night.

'The sounds of him taking a shower in "our" bathroom confirmed my worst fears. What was I to do? Call home to mother? Run? What? Finally he came out of the bathroom wearing nothing but a towel and told me he was bushed and wanted to sleep. There was only one bedroom – still warm from my recent occupancy. I showed it to him and he climbed into bed. I fetched blankets from the closet, preparing to sleep on the couch. He asked me what I was doing. I told him and he said there's no need for that, and indicated the bed beside himself. It was all so "fait accompli". He obviously expected no arguments from me. I'm ashamed to say that I climbed meekly into bed and lay there expecting rape. Nothing of the kind. He was asleep! I didn't expect to sleep a wink that night, but must have because around dawn I woke to find him sitting on the bed looking at me. He told me he wanted me to come to Hollywood and that he had a picture in mind for me.

'I just lay there staring at him. I tried to tell myself that I was dreaming, that none of this was happening. I hoped, *if* this was real, that he would just go away. No such luck, but anyway, I did the call, did get to Hollywood and made a movie opposite a really great leading man. Even today I can't believe how Hughes treated me over the next few years. The picture I made took forever to be released and meanwhile I built myself quite a good career on loan-outs to other studios, but from time to time I still got that knock on the door.'

One extraordinary aspect of Hughes' love life is the number of ladies prepared to confess that they succumbed to 'that shambling, boyish charm' – not to mention the money and the power. At some time or another Lana Turner, Ava Gardner, Norma Shearer, Joan Fontaine and Veronica Lake, among others, all reported on their encounters with Hughes but one of the more bizarre concerned the most unlikely female star of them all – Bette Davis.

At the time Bette was married to an orchestra leader, Harmon Nelson, whose work kept him out most nights. Word reached Nelson that Hughes was laying siege to

Bette and, rumour had it, the defences were weakening. Suspicious that something was really going on Nelson had his apartment wired for sound. In those days, before tape machines, this was a complicated business and meant running wires from the concealed microphones to an adjoining apartment where a cumbersome recording machine was set up ready to preserve forever the sound emanating from the bedroom. Night after night a hired detective sat disconsolately by the machine and nothing happened. Nelson kept paying the fees so the man sat on. One night he hit pay dirt. Hughes was there in the apartment with Miss Davis and things 'were hotting up'. Harmon Nelson abandoned his baton and rushed to the apartment where the machine was set up. He was in time to hear unmistakable noises of passion between an apparently very patient Bette and the ardent Hughes. Finally when all passion was spent Nelson snatched up the wax disc that had recorded it all and rushed to his own apartment where he was in time to confront Hughes. The two men squared off to each other while Bette did the traditional screen heroine thing and started screaming. Hughes punched and missed, toppled over the furniture and lay there looking winded and foolish. Bette demanded of her husband what he wanted – divorce? Nelson shook his head. What he wanted was $75,000 for the recording which Hughes knew to contain some explicit discussion on his personal sex problems, variously rumoured to be a) impotence, b) premature ejaculation, c) a liking for being tied up and having his testicles threatened with a cut-throat razor. Hughes bought the recording and went his way. As did Nelson the moment Bette got her breath back. It is said that she afterwards expunged the whole incident by paying Hughes back.

Late in the forties Hughes bought himself a studio –

RKO – and seemed set to become a conventional Holly-wood Mogul. It was about this time that the obsessional nature of the man started to become apparent. Having launched Jane Russell on her career by starring her in a so-so Western whose main features of interest were her daringly low-cut blouses and racy dialogue, Hughes cut it and re-cut it for four solid years, to try to create some measure of interest in a lukewarm public. Finally he hit on the idea that nothing was better for a movie than bad publicity. He personally financed a campaign to get his own picture banned. The resultant publicity – one unfor-tunate theatre owner got himself arrested – did get the public's interest and they flocked to see this 'daring' movie.

Hughes' acquisition of RKO was of particular interest to one young and beauteous RKO star. Jane Greer had once been under contract to Hughes. She thought she had escaped into the 'real' world when she got a contract with RKO only to wake one morning to find that Hughes had bought the studio, and her contract. She was horrified at the realization that he was, once again, her boss. She dreaded the inevitable call to his office, maintained per-versely on the Samuel Goldwyn lot and not at RKO. There are those who say he never saw the RKO studios and that his sole reason for buying the troubled studio was to regain 'possession' of Jane Greer. True or not, at their meeting Hughes made it clear that now he 'owned' her he would expect her to be available when and where he wanted. Jane spiritedly pointed out that she was newly married and had no intention of rejoining the Howard Hughes convenience sex machine. Hughes countered this by promising her that unless she fell into line, he would ensure that she would never work again. She would serve out her contract, on full pay, but there would be no pictures and no publicity. He reminded her that she had five years to go on her present contract and that unless she 'saw sense' and made herself available to him the public would forget her and her career, from that moment forward, was finished.

Jane politely thanked him for continuing her salary but repeated that she had no intention of 'seeing sense'.

Both kept their word. Hughes, always diffident, couldn't accept rejection. He spent a fortune over many years trying to find a 'new' Jane Greer. Hundreds of girls were screened, dozens of them tested. His first serious contender was a beautiful girl, Faith Domergue, who happened to be fifteen years old. He kept her under contract for four years before launching her in a $4 million picture called *Vendetta*. Hughes spent a further four years in his usual cutting routine before releasing it to a totally uninterested public. Meanwhile Hughes had turned his attentions to a girl found by his avid talent hunters, and reputed to be like Jane Greer's twin sister. This was a girl called Joan Dickson, for whom Hughes had high hopes. Unfortunately Miss Dickson didn't have the talent so nothing, finally, came of it.

Meanwhile Hughes' obsessions grew deeper. His talent spies reported on an English actress, auburn haired and busty, the way Hughes liked them. Hughes had her investigated and found the young lady was under contract to the J Arthur Rank Organisation in London, and already had some very creditable starring roles behind her. The girl's name was Jean Simmons, and she was anxious to marry an equally attractive young British actor, Stewart Granger, who was then working in Hollywood. Jean came out for the wedding and woke up to find that Hughes had bought her contract from J Arthur Rank. At first she was pleased. This meant that she could stay in Hollywood, close to her new husband, and everything looked lovely. Coming from England she was unaware of

Hughes' attitude to those he had under contract. At their first meeting, on the back seat of a battered Chevrolet, she was confronted with Hughes' blunt suggestions as to how she could best further her career.

Horrified, the young actress reported this conversation to her new husband. Granger, who did know Hughes' reputation reacted angrily and consulted his best friend, a fellow British actor called Michael Wilding, who was then about to marry the equally brunette and busty Elizabeth Taylor. Wilding had cause to hate Hughes and together they cooked up a plot, worthy of only the corniest of B-pictures, to kill Hughes!

The idea was that Jean Simmons should call up Hughes and imply that she had decided to play things his way. Jean was to invite Hughes to visit the matrimonial home which overlooked a precipitous cliff with a clear drop to rocks below. Jean was to 'lure' Hughes out onto the terrace to admire the view where the outraged husband, played by Stewart Granger, would discover Hughes making overtures to his wife and push him over the cliff edge.

Fortunately for everyone involved this plan was never put into execution. What did happen was that Jean was cast in a series of pictures which, in retrospect, seem to have been designed to ruin her career. Hughes hired well known actor-bully Otto Preminger as director and instructed him to give Jean Simmons as 'hard a time as you damn well can'.

Hell knew no fury like Howard Hughes spurned!

Obsessional interest in one particular young woman has been the downfall of many a producer. When that obsession is genuine love then there is no hope for him. Nothing stands in the way. Such a fate was about to befall David O Selznick when he was approached in New York by an agent anxious to promote the career of a promising young actor. The actor was Robert Walker, but Selznick's eye strayed beyond Walker to his beautiful young wife Phyllis. Phyllis had just given birth to their second child and was starting to get restless being plain Mrs Walker. She had previously made a couple of unnoticed movies with Republic before marrying the rising young actor and on meeting Selznick those ambitions were revived.

Selznick let the young mother know that if she were to present herself at his Hollywood offices, she might well learn that all was not lost in her moribund career. Selznick's interest in Mrs Phyllis Walker was obviously reciprocated since she left for Hollywood within a few months, and presented herself to Selznick's casting director, Katherine Brown. Katherine Brown was already well aware of Selznick's 'special interest' but mystified by his attempts to dupe her into believing he wasn't sure who this 'unknown girl' was. By July 1941 he was deliberately misnaming her in memos – pretending to confuse Phyllis Walker with Phyllis Thaxter, an established Broadway actress – and then pretending shock at the prospect of signing 'a girl who has done nothing' to a contract starting at $200 a week. Phyllis Walker was renamed Jennifer Jones and Selznick began a campaign to make her accept able in the title role of *Claudia*. A test he shot of his live-in protégée was shown to the author of the novel on which the movie was to be based, Rose Franken, who made clear her strong negative reaction. Selznick, who only two months previously had pretended not to know her name, was in September 1942 replying to Rose Franken with a fierce defence of Jennifer Jones. Selznick had wanted Cary Grant to play the male lead but his insistence that Jennifer Jones was to be Claudia caused Cary Grant to walk. The movie was postponed. Jennifer Jones had been under contract, and heavily promoted, for a year without working when a reluctant Selznick loaned her out to Twentieth Century-Fox for *The Song of Bernadette*. Jennifer triumphed, winning her Oscar against the other Selznick nominee, Ingrid Bergman.

There is one story from the production of *The Song of Bernadette* which throws an interesting light on the psyche of Hollywood at this time. The movie features a brief but important appearance of the Virgin Mary at Lourdes and much discussion took place inside Fox about whether the Virgin should be seen and, if seen, who could play the part without risking risible charges of blasphemy. It was decided that the problem should be referred to Darryl F Zanuck, who, while still head of production, was overseas in the army. Zanuck, thinking such matters trivial in the face of his contribution to the salvation of democracy, treated the matter accordingly and cabled back a suggestion he thought so ridiculous that even his studio executives would see it for the joke it was intended to be. Zanuck's suggestion was Linda Darnell. His sense of humour failing him, Henry Kind, the director, did just that and Linda duly played the sexiest vision of the Virgin that has ever been. Hollywood, on hearing the news, fell about laughing and the scene was hastily and hazily reshot.

The release of the movie was long delayed for substantial re-editing but when it finally emerged Selznick was puffed with pride that Jennifer Jones had triumphantly justified his faith in her. Jennifer, feeling that she had arrived, filed for divorce from the long-suffering Robert Walker, while Selznick sought to clear the decks of their troubled romance by seeking divorce from his wife Irene, who happened to be Louis B Mayer's daughter. Jennifer's divorce went smoothly enough but Selznick's was to prove trickier, and it wasn't until July 1949 that they were finally able to marry.

Meanwhile, what of Robert Walker? He shared two

children with Jennifer and, briefly, a small house in Hollywood, after coming out at her behest. The reunion didn't work and the affair with Selznick continued. Acquiescing in divorce for the sake of Jennifer's career paid off for Walker when Selznick brought him to co-star with Jennifer in a war-time weepie called *Since You Went Away*. This pay-off was a double-edged sword for Walker, since while playing love scenes with his wife he watched at the end of the day as she went home with the producer. His character, ever fragile, couldn't take it and he started seeking solace in ever-deeper bottles. The strain of playing love scenes with Walker also told on Jennifer, who several times fled the set and had to be coaxed weeping from her dressing room to carry on.

Retrospectively, the casting of Walker to play opposite his wife by usurper Selznick was seen as an exquisitely sadistic thing to do. It certainly ruined any prospect Walker had of building himself a career independent of Jennifer, whose walk-out now became an obsession with him. The drinking bouts got worse, and his constant accusations against Selznick and Jennifer got to be a major cause for concern.

Through his alcoholic haze Walker was, somehow, managing to build himself a reputation as a fine young actor. *Strangers on a Train* for Hitchcock had him playing a character planning to murder his wife, which must have been close to his own personal feelings at the time. What he couldn't have known was that *someone* was planning to murder *him* in real life.

In September 1951 Walker returned home from a drinking binge – by this time he was rarely ever completely sober – to find a doctor waiting to give him a 'sedative' injection. This sedative was sodium amytal which, taken with alcohol, can prove fatal. Walker knew this and resisted, even saying precisely, 'You can't give me that, I've been drinking! It'll kill me!' The doctor summoned two attendants to hold Walker down while the injection was given. Three hours later Robert Walker, aged thirty-four, was dead. The coroner's inquest concluded that Walker had died of 'alcoholism' and the doctor was cleared.

David O Selznick's own career as a maverick independent became confused and lost. He lost confidence in himself, and sought co-producers with whom to share the risks. Jennifer was sent off to Europe for *Gone to Earth*, which failed, and then into another co-production, *Terminal Station*, which did indeed prove to be the end of the line for Selznick. Twentieth chipped in with finance for one last try, *A Farewell to Arms*, but when that too bombed out Selznick all but gave up. He died of a heart attack in 1965, aged sixty-three.

9
The Fifties – Invasion of the One-eyed Monsters

With the dawn of the fifties the Hollywood Moguls were all still in place. These were the men who had practically invented the medium, developed it and shaped it in their own image. Some of their hired help had been shaken and driven abroad by the McCarthy hearings but they had emerged unscathed. There were new, heavier, taxes to pay, but in compensation they had regained their European markets and once more dominated world film making. With huge financial resources, contracts with every major star and vast tracts of real estate, what could challenge their established kingdoms? Television . . .?

For ageing Moguls who had yet to master the technical intricacies of the sixty-year-old movie camera, the electronic 'miracle' of television was simply a jungle in which they got promptly lost.

Not understanding it, even less the threat it posed, they determined to have nothing to do with it. When they couldn't ignore it they ridiculed it. *Will Success Spoil Rock Hunter?* was a Broadway comedy that was bought by Hollywood specifically to ridicule the emerging rival. A scene was brazenly inserted in which the male star, Tony Randall, takes time out to directly address the audience on just how 'ridiculous' this impudent newcomer was.

When TV continued to make inroads the Moguls turned their minds to evaluating what they had that TV didn't. The most obvious answer, in those early days, was colour. Colour, thought of until this time as only suitable for Westerns and musicals, now became standard.

Darryl Zanuck at Twentieth Century-Fox remembered

a Frenchman who had been around Hollywood years before trying to peddle a new anamorphic screen system and instigated a search to find him. Bausch and Lomb developed the lenses and CinemaScope was brought into the fight. Others came up with aged gimmicks such as Cinerama, a tryptych screen first used in the 1920s; 3-D and higher definition lenses. In fact anything that TV didn't have.

The Moguls were confused and growing increasingly desperate. These were the same men who had resisted the introduction of sound as 'extravagant', but they also remembered that there were other, previously dismissed, 'nuts' around town with equally outlandish suggestions. Finally they stumbled across the one thing which the anodyne TV didn't have and which they had in abundance – sex!

Subjects that had previously not been mentioned in the hearing of the Hays Office, were hastily dusted off and put into production. *From Here To Eternity* scored many firsts but the front runner at creating controversy was an old Hollywood hand – Otto Preminger. He threw two hats into the ring: *The Moon is Blue* which brought such previously banned words as 'virgin' and 'pregnant' to the screen, and the first film to deal openly with the drug addiction of its hero, *The Man with the Golden Arm*. Both pictures were made without the blessing of the Hays Office and both were put into distribution without its MPPA (Motion Picture Producers Association) seal of approval. Fans flocked to the few theatres brave enough to risk prosecution by showing these films in such numbers that the major theatre chains were forced into breaking their long-standing agreements and letting these outspoken pictures play on their prestigious screens. Preminger had made a beachhead onto which poured every other producer looking for salvation.

Nobody in Hollywood was less surprised than Zanuck at Twentieth Century-Fox. He had first appreciated the value of a 'strong' controversial picture back in the thirties when, against fierce studio opposition, he had made a politically controversial movie of *The Grapes of Wrath*. In the forties he, a non-Jew, had produced *Gentlemen's Agreement*, an exposé of anti-Semitism. The following year he had essayed *Pinky*, with Jeanne Craine as a mulatto girl trying to cross the racial frontiers of the day and pass as white. What better then than combining sex with colour and making an all-black version of *Carmen*? Preminger was Zanuck's first choice as director and the project was put into work. Harry Belafonte was the automatic choice for the male but the question all Hollywood was asking was who was to play the title role?

Whoever it was she was going to have to be black, beautiful and a singer. The obvious answer was Lena Horne and around town that came to be the general assumption. But there was another candidate that nobody but herself saw as a possibility – Dorothy Dandridge. Dorothy had been around town a long time. Starting out in the black Los Angeles ghetto of Watts, she had been a child extra and played small walk-ons in dozens of pictures, among them *A Day at the Races* with the Marx Brothers, as well as going the rounds of cabarets with various singing acts. Her first real part in pictures had been as a jungle princess in a Lex Barker Tarzan picture, but apart from that she seemed destined, at thirty-three, to succeed Hetty McDaniel and play nothing but coloured maids.

A low-budget picture, *Bright Road*, with Harry Belafonte had brought her some critical notice and fired Dorothy with the notion of going after *Carmen Jones*.

Dorothy had two great handicaps in her career. First she had married young and been abandoned by her husband who left her with a brain-damaged child.

Secondly, she was heavily sexually inhibited which ruled out the more traditional roads to Hollywood success. Dorothy took stock of herself and decided that she was at the point of no return. Either she went for it this time or forgot it. Her manager approached Preminger with his suggestion of Dorothy for Carmen. Preminger was aware of her from having screened *Bright Road* and not unreceptive. He wanted her, though, for the lesser good-girl part of Cindy-Lou. Dorothy was outraged. She got a face-to-face meeting with Preminger and pleaded her cause. Preminger was unimpressed. Her image, he told her, was that of a stand-offish lady; a kind of black Loretta Young. 'Never,' he told her, 'could you play a whore!'

Dorothy left Preminger's office fuming with rage. She went home, took off her underwear, slit a tight black skirt to the thigh, put on whorish make-up and forced her way back into Preminger's office and, interrupting a conference meeting, raised one leg high onto a chair, so giving the startled director an opportunity to note her absence of underwear, and stared directly into his flustered face. Preminger demanded to know what she thought she was doing. Dorothy told him she was there 'to prove I can be a whore'. Dorothy got the part, which proved sensational, and also the director. Dorothy and Otto enjoyed many a long conference for many years afterwards uninterrupted by her other affairs – always with white men – and marriages.

After *Carmen Jones* Dorothy's career took off. She was a genuine star and making big money with her nightclub appearances. The problem for Twentieth Century and Zanuck, who now had her under contract, was finding the right vehicle for her. It was three years before they reunited her with Harry Belafonte for *Island in the Sun* in which Zanuck found a new area of controversy – an interracial romance between Dorothy and British actor John

Justin. Even though this picture was to prove a huge box-office success Twentieth still didn't know what to do with her. MGM put her into *The Decks Ran Red*, but even a rape scene with Stuart Whitman couldn't save it, and the ship sank with all hands. The same year a heavier, sexier part with Curt Jurgens in a slave ship picture *Tamango* seemed to offer a better prospect. Dorothy played her scenes with the lustful Captain, Jurgens, with such enthusiasm that a cooler version had to be shot for domestic consumption. American audiences were not yet ready to accept heavy breathing across the racial lines. Salvation came again from her long-time lover Preminger, who called her back to Hollywood for Goldwyn's lavish *Porgy and Bess*, for which she was to win a Golden Globe award.

Throughout this rise Dorothy had been conducting a number of affairs – one was with Peter Lawford – but her most persistent admirer of all was a restaurateur, Jack Dennison. It was he who pursued her to Spain where she went to make *Malaga* with Trevor Howard. It was there that he convinced her that the world was ready for her to marry a white man. On her return to Los Angeles Dorothy announced her forthcoming marriage for June 1959. The marriage was a disaster for Dorothy's career. A deniable affair was one thing; an undeniable interracial marriage something else. Hollywood turned its back and she never made another movie. By 1963 she was forced into bankruptcy and the following year was found dead in her West Hollywood apartment. How she died was never established with any certainty. There were two inquests. The first found that she had died of a rare embolism, the second that she had taken an overdose of an anti-depressant drug, but whether the overdose had been deliberate or accidental was never determined.

* * *

No greater contrast to the diffident Dorothy could be imagined than Jayne Mansfield. Destined forever to play, both on and offscreen, the archetypal dumb blonde, Jayne was a very intelligent lady. Married at sixteen, a mother at seventeen, Jayne nevertheless graduated from high school and was accepted into the University of Texas. Determined to regain her figure after giving birth Jayne started serious work on her body. She found that she could do almost anything she wanted with it – it just took guts and determination. Those she had in plenty. Her spectacular forty-one-inch bust enabled her to supplement her income by posing at some of the most heavily attended life classes the art department of the university could ever remember. Her husband, Paul Mansfield, was meanwhile drafted and gone from his young family for two years. When he came marching home it was to find Jayne packed and fired with ambition to go to Hollywood. Paul didn't like the idea but it was that or nothing.

Jayne loved Hollywood even when it failed to reciprocate. She saw early that the most essential thing was to be noticed. She began helping out a public relations man who, in lieu of salary, started pointing her in the right directions.

One of his firsts stunts on her behalf was to get her an invitation to attend the premiere of a film by Howard Hughes' star, Jane Russell. Jane had just completed *Underwater* which featured the famed Russell bosom barely contained within a skin-tight swimsuit. Jayne considered her assets even more attractive and she, and her PR mentor, devised a strategy for the premiere, which was to be held underwater in a swimming pool.

It was pure media hype. It was to be Jane Russell's night and probably would have been but for Jayne. She shrewdly timed her entrance to the pool five minutes before Jane's. The press photographers took one look at the big blonde in the tiny bikini and started popping off their flash bulbs. The photographers went wild when the simpering blonde dived into the water to surface, having 'accidentally' lost the top half of her swimsuit. The flashing of bulbs lit up the night. By the time the star of the evening, Jane, appeared, the photographers had run out of film so the following day it was the 'unknown' Jayne who got all the publicity.

Warners, envious of Twentieth's Marilyn Monroe, snapped her up. Unfortunately Jayne's dramatic talents didn't match her ability to attract publicity. They threw her away in small parts and walk-ons and then dropped her contract at first renewal. Her agent, Bill Shifrin, had the inside track on a play about to be produced on Broadway, *Will Success Spoil Rock Hunter?* and knew they were looking for a girl to send up Marilyn. He sent Jayne east and she walked right into a Broadway smash hit, which ran for over a year.

Warners, furious at themselves for failing to spot her comedic talent, wanted her back, but found that Twentieth had got there first. They bought up *Rock Hunter* – a thinly disguised rewrite of a true Marilyn escapade – and, just beginning to have trouble with the original, brought in Jayne to threaten her. Jayne shared one thing with Marilyn – her exhibitionism. However, the two girls couldn't have been more different. Jayne saw her body as a sure-fire means of getting press coverage while Marilyn's exhibitionism was simply a means of letting her true self out to take over from the bewildering screen persona that seemed to have taken residence in her body.

Twentieth, on the principle that two heads were better than one, started Jayne on a career that was a mirror-image of Marilyn's. Marilyn had made *The Seven Year Itch*, Jayne made *The Girl Can't Help It*. Marilyn's *Bus Stop* was followed by Jayne's *The Wayward Bus*. When *Kiss Them For Me* failed as a vehicle for Jayne, Fox saw that the joke had gone sour and gladly lent her out to independents. In England she raised a B-feature night-club-and-mobster plot to feature status. This was *Too Hot to Handle* in which she parodied her own parody. The censors objected to her revealing gowns and an animator had to be employed to paint sequins over Jayne's bare nipples, already immortalized on the negative.

Twentieth had, meanwhile failed to pick up her option. Towards the end of the fifties Jayne – and Marilyn's – busty blatant sexiness was going out of fashion. Jayne went to that salvation of many a busty blonde, Rome. There, with her career desperately plummeting, she threw herself into the night life of a city that seemed to appreci-ate her as Hollywood had failed to do. From Rome she went to Greece and then back to Rome where she resorted to more and more desperate stunts to keep her assets in newsprint. A supposed shipwreck with Jayne 'missing' for eighteen hours drew no more than a yawn. Jayne startled two Roman floorwaiters by staging an exclusive, and total, strip-tease for them in the privacy of her own suite. Having assuaged their roused passions she sent them off after getting a promise that they would tell the paparazzi all about their good fortune. They did but nobody believed a word of it. Annoyed at their failure to light up the late editions, Jayne restaged the whole incident, this time with the paparazzi present. Nobody cared.

Jayne had, by this time, taken refuge in the bottle and things started going from bad to worse. There is much talk of two movies, supposedly hard-core porn, which she made in Rome, but since neither seems to have surfaced this has to be treated with some scepticism. It is more likely that Jayne herself started the rumours of hard-core pictures just to gain news coverage she by now desperately needed.

When Marilyn died Jayne had expected to inherit her mantle and stood by for the 'call'. It never came. With Marilyn, died the entire idea of the dyed blonde with the heaving bosom.

It all came to a sickening end when, in June 1967, when she was on the way to a cabaret date in New Orleans, her car rounded a bend on a slick road and sliced into a parked agricultural truck. Jayne and the driver, husband-of-the-time Sam Brody, were decapitated. Jayne, at thirty-four, got the publicity she coveted for the last time.

Howard Hughes was still alive and well in the fifties. His nation-wide team of talent spotters were having to find younger and younger girls to fill the needs of the increasingly eccentric tycoon. Mamie van Doren was spotted by one of them in a newspaper photograph when she was fifteen. Hughes gazed at the burgeoning talent and nodded. Mamie was put under contract to Hughes and given a one-line part in a picture he was then making with Janet Leigh and John Wayne, *Jet Pilot*. This picture, shot in 1950, suffered from the usual Hughes prevarications and inability to finish anything and Miss van Doren's immortal one-line part wasn't screened until 1957, by which time both the jet aircraft featured in the story and busty blondes were obsolete. Hughes pursued Mamie as he pursued each and every other young girl under contract. An invitation to Palm Springs for a weekend was his usual ploy. The girl invited was carefully primed on what was expected of her and warned not to waste Hughes' valuable time, or incidentally, jeopardize the Executive Pimp's job. Mamie took her mother along on the Palm Springs command performance weekend and this, apparently, dampened Hughes' ardour. Not so fortunate was another busty fifteen-year-old blonde who, like Mamie, took her mother but couldn't avoid finding herself naked in Hughes' bed. Matters were coming to a head when the bedroom door burst open and an irate Mom stood there demanding to know what Hughes thought he was doing. A hurried conference between breathless mother, daughter and Hughes resulted in a settlement for $250,000. Maybe this girl's Mom had the right idea since Mamie's continued virtue did nothing for her career with Hughes' company. At twenty she switched to Paramount who, unfortunately, saw her as nothing more than another dumb blonde and cast her accordingly.

Hughes sold out of the movie business in 1957 and secretly married long-time contractee Jean Peters who moved with him into total seclusion. What happened to the other hundreds of girls under contract is not documented.

Pier Angeli was brought from Italy, along with her sister Marisa Pavan, to play in Fred Zinneman's *Teresa* – the story of the problems facing Italian-born GI brides. The movie was a critical success, as was the delicately beautiful Pier, but did little to disturb box office torpor. The same year she made *The Light Touch* with much the same results. Hollywood, which had started her at the top, rapidly lost interest. Pier's confusion at this turn of events led her into a romance with the new boy in town, James Dean. Having been ruled out of military service because he was gay, Dean found instant stardom with *East of Eden*. Tormented, anguished personalities like his had been made fashionable by Marlon Brando. His off-screen personality was much the same. Rude, offensive, mostly unwashed and unshaven, he seemed hell bent on self-destruction. Whatever there was about him for Pier Angeli to love was known only to herself. Momma Angeli was horrified at the affair and Pier was forced to marry singer Vic Damone. The marriage was a predictable fiasco and when Dean's self-destructiveness finally culminated in a road crash in 1956 Pier was totally crushed. Marriage with Damone ended and Pier started to find work again. In 1960 she made *The Angry Silence* and that was about the end of it. Still very beautiful, she ended her confusion in 1971 with an overdose, having written to a friend that she couldn't bear the thought of being forty.

Two totally contrasting blondes came to Hollywood in the fifties: High Society Grace Kelly, graduate of the US Academy of Dramatic Art, and Kim Novak, once voted Miss Deepfreeze. Both were to suffer at the hands of the increasingly eccentric Alfred Hitchcock, Kim in Hitchcock's *Vertigo*, Grace three times in *Dial M for Murder, Rear Window* and *To Catch a Thief*. Grace's career was to be cut short when she quit Hollywood to marry Prince Rainier, but she managed to pick up an Oscar for trying to rescue Bing Crosby from alcohol. Kim was contracted to Harry Cohn, who was desperately searching for a new star he could claim to have created after Rita Hayworth had walked out on him. It is obvious what Hitchcock saw in both ladies – they shared, for different reasons, a slightly glacial look and that was what Hitchcock most wanted in a woman. Admire them he didn't. His penchant for wishing to degrade ladylike blondes was a well known casting hazard in Hollywood. He had a fascination for toilet bowls – bathrooms loom large in all Hitchcock's pictures – and a penchant for shooting tests of glacial blondes squatting on them. Enduring both of these was a somewhat embarrassing consequence of winning a title role in his movies. Rape scenes and bloody violence towards women also make material for the interested psychologist. What he used to attract the continued loyalty of Grace Kelly is a subject of much gossip in Hollywood. Certainly she was not above pandering to his voyeuristic impulses, which were one of his more harmless traits. His truly sadistic tendencies reveal themselves on screen, culminating in his treatment of Tippi Hedren in

The Birds when the successor to Grace found herself in danger of being blinded by the attentions of the frantically pecking birds who were playing the title role. Both the birds and Miss Hedren were pinned to the ground to add 'authenticity', and it is a close-run thing to decide who was the more panic-stricken.

Meanwhile Harry Cohn, who thought he had found a nice compliant girl in Kim Novak, soon found he had on his hands a stubborn woman quite capable of fighting her corner. First signed at $150 a week, she had clawed her way up to stardom but was still only getting $750. Her anger at this salary, which she considered inadequate, was further increased when she discovered that Harry Cohn was demanding $100,000 (of which Miss Novak would get not one cent) from Otto Preminger for a loan-out to *The Man with the Golden Arm*. Later she found that her co-star in *Jeanne Engels*, Jeff Chandler, was getting $200,000 against her own $15,000. Kim decided to take on Harry Cohn. As a first move she changed agents and took suspension. Cohn was sure she couldn't hold out, but she did and finally forced Cohn into submitting to her agent's demands. Kim moved to a salary scale more in line with her earning power at the time and Columbia went back to what passed for normal. However, Cohn's problems were far from over. In December 1956 he was in New York when he learned that Kim was having an affair with Sammy Davis Jnr. Cohn responded by having a heart attack. Kim was then Columbia's highest-earning asset and Cohn, under pressure from his stockholders, saw the liaison with the black singer as an acute threat to her status. Cohn called in some outstanding favours from Chicago associates who sought out Sammy Davis in Las Vegas where he was appearing. Various accounts of what happened behind those closed doors abound, ranging from offers of a Quiet Funeral among the surrounding sand dunes, to a threat to his professional life. Whatever was said it was highly effective since, within weeks, Sammy had married Loray White, a black dancer.

Jean Seberg was another to suffer from the racial intolerance of the day. She had been plucked from her Iowa college to debut in the title role in Preminger's *Saint Joan*. Completely without experience of professional acting or the predatory ways of Hollywood's Moguls, Jean found herself on Preminger's casting couch in a state of bewilderment. That same air of bewildered naïvety she brought to the role of Saint Joan, who was anything but naïve and bewildered. The movie died and Jean, through no fault of her own, suffered personal abuse, much of it because a complete newcomer had been brought in to play such a coveted role. *Bonjour Tristesse* did little more for her but did introduce her to France. There Jean-Luc Godard's *A Bout de Souffle* (*Breathless*) rescued her from the scrap heap her previous performances were directing her towards. Free of the bullying, demanding Preminger, Jean enjoyed a brief flowering of talent. The freewheeling radical circles in which she moved in Paris, after marrying novelist Romain Gary, roused her interest in politics, and led her to involvement with the Black Panther movement. This attracted the attention of J Edgar Hoover, head of the FBI. He sent out orders to his men to 'get' Jean Seberg any way they could. Hoover couldn't stomach having St Joan leading what he saw as a serious threat of insurrection. Malicious press items started appearing about the 'true' nature of Jean's interest in the black radical movement and more particularly her personal relationship with its leader, Malcolm X. These rumours climaxed with planted hints that Jean's pregnancy had resulted from such a relationship and that the baby would be born black. Jean broke under the strain, which led her, after the baby was still-born, to have its tiny body exposed to public view in a glass coffin to show the world that the baby was indeed white. While this proved the critics wrong it also caused a great deal of revulsion among the mothers of America who couldn't understand the pressures which had led Jean to such extremes. Jean took to barbiturates and increasingly erratic behaviour. She divorced Gary, married twice more, but was virtually broken. She finally ended her agony in September 1979, so closing her totally confused life.

In 1957 an event occurred which is unique in the history of the Hollywood casting couch – and the girl herself remains, to this day, ignorant of what nearly happened. John Wayne and John Huston were in Japan looking for a girl to co-star opposite Wayne in *The Barbarian and the Geisha*. They wanted a girl who would combine both Oriental and Occidental ideas of beauty. Having exhausted the possibilities of the professional Japanese actresses they lighted upon the idea of extending their search to the delightful geisha houses themselves. Enthusiastically they set out into Tokyo's nightlife. One night they found just what they were looking for – a girl beautiful to both Eastern and Western eyes. They started negotiations with the geisha mistress, who was horrified. She pointed out that the young girl was not yet a fully trained geisha but merely a maiko, a trainee. The geisha houses spend a great deal of time and money in perfecting their candidates' skills in the art of tea pouring, and before a girl can graduate from maiko to geisha she must find a sponsor willing to reimburse the house.

It is now generally understood in the West that the traditional Geisha is not a prostitute, the skills she sells being social rather than sexual. What is less well known is the system known as 'pillow money'. The sponsor willing to finance the girl's graduation is entitled to take the girl's carefully preserved virginity and to enjoy three nights with the girl during which she demonstrates how well she has learned the theoretical art of love.

Huston and Wayne were intrigued by this new knowledge but both realized that such a graduation in the bed of two eminent Westerners would not remain unknown to the press. They paid the pillow money but declined the 'reward'. They left the house confident that they had secured their Oriental co-star.

Unfortunately they had not taken account of the Japanese regard for observing all ritual in its minutest detail. By paying the pillow money and refusing the girl they had disgraced both the girl and the house. The geisha mistress responded by removing all traces of her disgrace. The confused girl was packed off back to her village and her name struck from the geisha records. They further refused all Huston's pleas to bring the girl back or tell him where she could be found.

So, somewhere in Northern Japan, is one Japanese woman unaware of the unique position she occupies in the history of the casting couch. For although she was willing, she lost her chance at movie stardom and a total change of life because neither the star nor the director was willing to go to bed with her!

Less honourable was a tragic incident during the filming of *The Alamo* – Wayne's self-financed bid, in vain, for an Oscar. John Wayne was consistent in one thing – his love for the Latin-type beauty. On location for *The Alamo* there were many examples of the beautiful Latin among the girl extras. One of them was a girl called La Jeanne Ethridge. She had been cast from a Hollywood workshop theatre where she and her boyfriend, Chester Harvey Smith, worked out. Chester was along on the shoot too and the shared $150 dollars a week was most welcome.

Wayne's eye fell upon Ethridge and during a break in

shooting she was flattered when the 'Duke' stopped by to chat over their coffee. Later that day an assistant informed her that Wayne would like to continue their conversation over drinks at his location hotel. Wise in the ways of Hollywood, and at twenty-seven no wide-eyed innocent, La Jeanne happily accepted. Less happy with the arrangement was Chester Harvey Smith, who noted his girl's overnight absence. The following morning, on set, Chester sought her out and asked what was happening. La Jeanne told him that she was 'making a career move' that would benefit them both. Chester seemed to accept this for the moment but, later, when Wayne promoted La Jeanne from walk-on extra to small speaking parts – her salary going from $75 a week to $350 – he started to get restless. The next day he heard from someone else that La Jeanne was being moved out of the extras' accommodation in the tiny rail town of Spofford to Bracketville, which was both closer to the location and to Wayne. Chester got mad. He walked off the set and went to the ranch bunkhouse where he and La Jeanne had been housed. They rowed violently. La Jeanne told him that he was now a back number while she had moved into the Hollywood 'A' set. Chester blew his top and pulled the knife which the movie company had thoughtfully provided him with and stabbed La Jeanne to death.

John Wayne had personally financed the movie and its cost – high for those days at $12 million – left him more than just broke. A scandal during shooting could have been the death-knell. It might have been in any other State but Texas. Here was Wayne, boosting the local economies by millions in making a picture close to every Texan's heart. Instead of investigations, the clean-up squad went to work. Wayne's name was kept out of it, and almost no public mention of the murder was allowed.

Smith's preliminary arraignment was held in secret and

although Wayne was finally subpoenaed to the trial there was, uniquely, no jury. Instead, plea-bargaining had Smith pleading guilty in exchange for a twenty-year prison term in place of the death sentence Texas usually dealt out in such cases.

Wayne escaped immediate scandal in Texas but his publicity campaign for the picture and the Oscars left a bad taste around the prestigious ceremony which lingers even today. Overblown publicity, grandiose claims that suggested that anyone who didn't like *The Alamo* was being unpatriotic soured the members of the Academy who voted on the awards. The end result was that the only Oscar garnered by *The Alamo* was a grudging award for Best Sound.

Towards the end of the fifties Hollywood was changed. Television stalked the land and could no longer be dismissed. It was making serious inroads into the old order that had prevailed since movies had begun. While television threatened the Hollywood edifice the grim reaper gathered in those pioneers who had built it. Harry Cohn, Louis B Mayer, Jesse Lasky, William Randolph Hearst, William Fox, Erich von Stroheim. De Mille died, and Gary Cooper, Tyrone Power, Humphrey Bogart and Errol Flynn. There was one jaunty survivor, however: Darryl F Zanuck, a man who could be relied on to keep the old flag flying as long as was possible.

The start of the fifties had proved traumatic for Zanuck. At the 1950 Cannes Film Festival he had first met a young girl, Bella Weiger.

Zanuck's first sight of her came in the Cannes Casino. Bella was in Cannes supported by a consortium of newspapermen who were enjoying her embraces on a rota system. There was little to distinguish her from the other Festival call-girls but her exceptional beauty and the confident way she carried herself. On closer acquaintance

Zanuck was to realize that this was no mindless bimbo, but a self-educated intelligent girl who spoke four languages with fluency and subtlety. She was worlds removed from the ambitious young girls that Zanuck took, used and disposed of with such easy grace in the strictly observed ritual of the Hollywood casting couch. Zanuck was a powerful studio chief, you were an aspiring contender for fame, ergo you were his for the asking. Zanuck may have thought that Bella was just one more in the long line of girls that he had known. He was attracted but he wasn't a man to cross the street for a beautiful girl, he expected them to do all the crossing.

For her part Bella had been told of Zanuck's power, which initially interested her little, and also of his wealth, which interested her a lot.

Originally of Polish-Jewish origin, Bella had come to live in the industrial wastelands of northeastern France with her parents when her father found work there. She ran away from home to Paris when she was fourteen. The year was 1940. Bella was already a fully formed woman and obviously no student of politics since this was the year the Germans were to conquer France.

Bella was picked up by a pimp the moment she stepped out of the train at the Gare du Nord. He offered her comfortable sanctuary while he prepared her for the life that was to become her profession. Bella was fortunate in some respects since he was able to introduce her at a particularly high level.

There was in the Rue Pigalle, until the reforms of the sixties, a particular hotel which was unusual in that its front door was at all times locked. The 'hotel' was a thinly veiled, lavishly furnished, high-class bordello protected by the police which, among other things, specialized in young girls.

A visitor to this establishment – the writer benefited

from a conducted tour of it in 1959 – was admitted by a uniformed maid. Conducted into what might have once been the dining room, he was comfortably seated, given a glass of passable champagne and presently joined by the reigning 'hostess'. After some seemingly casual but piercing questioning the hostess would summon a passing maid who would present the guest with a brochure in which were displayed the photographs of all the girls then present. Some indication of taste would be arrived at and the girl or girls would then join the table and a second glass of wine was poured. The hostess would then leave the company to their own conversation and return to circulation.

It was all very expensive and discreet. The full-bodied Bella thrived on it and was enjoying an affluent life-style undreamed of at home. Then the Germans occupied Paris.

Weiger was a name which sprang to the eye of the Gestapo, scanning the police records in the Paris Sûreté, and so Bella was picked up.

At Gestapo headquarters they found they had a raven-haired beauty on their hands and were more than a little reluctant to pass her on down through the machine which was already consuming other French Jews. Sexual relationships with non-Aryans were officially forbidden under the Nazi code but they made frequent exceptions in Bella's case. If the brothel on the Rue Pigalle had been Bella's college then life at Gestapo headquarters was to be her university. Bella confided in few people about this period of her life but there is one living woman whose friendship with Bella was based on common experience. This lady, now in her sixties, didn't meet Bella until after the war but she was, probably, the one person to whom Bella was ever totally truthful.

Bella's life at Gestapo headquarters was a sickening

nightmare but was to get worse. News of the beautiful young captive reached higher authority which insisted that she be fed into the 'system'. Bella went from one dispersal camp to another, each reluctant to let her go, until finally she came to Auschwitz. There she became an 'officers only' whore required to attend the orgies with which the camp's officers sought solace after a hard day striving towards the final solution. Bella was there because she had no choice, but spoke of her astonishment at the number of German army girls who attended such orgies voluntarily and with apparent joy. Whatever Bella had to do she did and, miraculously, survived, externally intact. What had been killed in her was any true sense of joy and fun. She knew how to simulate it, but never felt it. Only with other women could she find any emotional depth.

Zanuck saw a beautiful girl seemingly filled with the joys of life and probably thought she was worth an afternoon's diversion. He had little trouble in arranging a rendezvous some months later when, he imagined, they met again by chance.

Bella totally misread the situation. While Zanuck was applying his Hollywood standards on her, she imagined that a man of his vast sexual experience with some of the world's most beautiful women would be expecting more than just to bounce on her belly. She set about planning an erotic experience worthy of such a discriminating palate. She didn't realize that Zanuck's experience was mostly with girls who knew the Hollywood rules and pliantly and, for the most part, unimaginatively, did what they had to do and merely made the right noises.

When Zanuck finally walked into her Paris apartment he didn't know what had hit him. Bella came at him with a highly developed sense of the erotic to such an extent that Zanuck was overwhelmed. Knocking on fifty, Zanuck found, under Bella's expert hands, all the vigour and enthusiasm of his youth returning, cleansing his jaded palate. In fact he became convinced, after further meetings, that Bella was restoring his youth to him.

Bella, realizing that she had a generous and powerful catch on her hands, took great care to ingratiate herself with Darryl's wife, Virginia. The measure of her success came when the invitation to Hollywood came not from Zanuck but from Virginia!

Bella came to Hollywood enthused with both Darryl and Virginia's convictions that she could be groomed into stardom. Zanuck was in a position to give her the full treatment and used his position as head of Twentieth Century-Fox to see that she got it. Bella in return delivered what she knew best – erotic delight. There were few people in Hollywood not aware of Zanuck's obsession with this beautiful Frenchwoman so it is hardly possible that Virginia Zanuck didn't know the true nature of her husband's relationship with Bella. All Virginia, apparently, asked was that nothing should be done that would embarrass her in public. Some measure of this can be assumed from the fact that the Zanucks, husband and wife, lent half of each of their given names to Bella. Weiger was dropped in favour of Darvi – the first syllable from Darryl, the second from Virginia.

The renamed Bella Darvi was tried out in a couple of low-budget routine pictures: *Hell and High Water* and *The Ravers*. Both passed without anyone noticing Bella's small and totally ineffectual contributions. It was about this time, 1953, that Zanuck felt ready to launch his surefire answer to television – CinemaScope. The vehicle was to be *The Egyptian*, starring Marlon Brando, Jean Simmons and Gene Tierney. It would also launch the mainfeature career of Bella. The script read-through with director Michael Curtiz was a disaster. Brando heard Bella's desperate attempts to sound plausible in the role of a courtesan, Nefer, and walked. Edmund Purdom was brought in to replace Brando. Jean Simmons, an established actress from a comfortable background, couldn't resist cracking: 'Bella Darvi is an actress that "Nefer" was.'

The film, given this beginning, was a total disaster. Bella was devastated. She had started out on this relationship with a very low estimate of herself, expecting nothing more than a whore's pay. The combination of Darryl and Virginia Zanuck and the Twentieth Century-Fox machine build-up had created high expectations. Now the world seemed to be telling her that not only was she just a whore but also ridiculous. Bella wanted to flee Hollywood and all the derision being heaped upon her. Zanuck wouldn't hear of it. Even Virginia wanted her to stay and try again.

That chance never came. Virginia Zanuck had always tolerated Darryl's studio philanderings so long as the children didn't have it forced on them. The crunch came when Darryl visited Bella's room one night forgetting that his grown daughter Susan was sleeping in the next room. Bella was, in the French style, a very vocal lover and young Susan was treated to an X-rated radio show through the thin walls. The following morning she complained to Mother and Bella was, shortly, on her way back to Paris. For Bella this was something of a relief. She had never claimed any great talent, and had been unprepared for the way in which Hollywood would turn on anyone who got a big chance – which each and every girl in Hollywood thought should have been hers – and failed.

Bella was astonished when she realized that this six-thousand-mile separation was not the end of her affair with Zanuck. Far from cooling his ardour he discovered that the old wham-bang-thank-you-ma'am routine of the average Hollywood encounter was no longer enough. What he wanted was with Bella in Paris. He started spending more and more of his time in Europe and convinced himself that Europe was the place for him to make pictures – as an independent!

Bella's reputation in hard-headed Paris was that of the conquering woman with a compliant millionaire American docilely lavishing gifts and money on her. It was a status much admired in the Paris of the mid-fifties. Even more so in the chic circles of the fashionable lesbians where Bella found her only true satisfaction.

Bella had, not one but two Achilles' heels. The first was her preference for girls, and Darryl loathed any deviation from heterosexuality, and gambling. In common with most of her circle Bella's attitude to money was that it was to be spent or gambled away and, since she had an inexhaustible source at hand, that's precisely what she did.

Rumours reached Zanuck of Bella's love-life when he was absent and he hired a private detective who had little difficulty in confirming them. Zanuck cut off his regular visits and Bella lost her meal ticket.

Over the following few years Bella was, nevertheless, able to get Zanuck's help when her creditors became too pressing. Zanuck's appetite for Europe remained unabated as he tried to make movie stars out of Juliette Greco, Irina Demick and Genevieve Gilles, these efforts being more or less as doom-struck as his efforts with Bella.

Hollywood remembers Bella as a talentless girl on the make. Hollywood has known many less honest whores than Bella, and persevered with them longer. Bella's problem was that she was brought to the right place at the wrong time. The old studio system was crumbling as the old founder Moguls were either dead or fading. The accountants were taking over and they took no notice of personal interests. The books could no longer be balanced in bed.

If Bella lacked talent then it was hardly her fault. Emotion had been burned out of her at the hands of the Gestapo. She could simulate only one kind of passion and Twentieth Century-Fox didn't make that kind of movie.

Bella tried suicide in 1958, 1962, 1966, and 1968. Each time Zanuck, even though their affair was long ended, came to her rescue. In 1971 she again struck rock bottom but by this time Zanuck was deeply involved in a corporate struggle for control of his studio and an affair with his latest protégée Genevieve Gilles, and so ignored her desperate pleas.

Bella ended her fragile tenure on life in September 1971. Monte Carlo the place, gas the medium. Her decomposing corpse wasn't found until a week later. Bella would have expected nothing more. Graduating from the Gestapo can do that to a girl.

10
The Sixties – The Dinosaurs Are Dying

Hollywood's fight against television was all but lost at the start of the sixties. In 1950 there had been five million TV sets in the whole of the United States. By the end of the decade there were fifty million. Twenty-five per cent of all movie houses had closed their doors forever. Anti-trust legislation had stripped the studios of their chains of theatres and the studios themselves were becoming the entertainment divisions of various multinational companies. Curiously this newcomer depended heavily on the vast stocks of old movies that the studios had built up over the years. It is still feeding on them to this very day.

With the break-up of the studios the star system, and its concomitant talent build-up, died too. Now a career in movies had to be built piecemeal and the aspirant had to finance his or her own career development. Gone were the days when a few breathless afternoons on the right couch could ensure a long-term contract and build-up. No more could a beauty pageant winner rise from a couch with a career in hand. In the new order of things she was more likely to get one walk-on in one movie. The couch had slid from institutional status to, almost, a social courtesy.

Hollywood itself splintered and diffused. Zanuck had, in many ways, shown that movies could be shot outside the hallowed boundaries of Hollywood. More and more movies were shot on location abroad. More and more, Hollywood sought part-financing from co-producers.

One consequence of this was to give greater opportunities to foreign stars coming in as part of the 'package'.

There was another reason for the influx of European actresses – nudity. Hollywood had, in its search for something to give the public that they couldn't get from television, fallen back on the oldest showman's ploy of all – the girls would have to take their clothes off.

At first there was great doubt about whether audiences would accept home-grown American girls playing nude scenes and this gave opportunities to the less-inhibited European girls. Anita Ekberg and Gia Scala were brought in to supply the bare flesh for *Four From Texas*. The first home-grown talent to bare all was Natalie Wood – a former child actress – who rose naked from a bath in Elia Kazan's *Splendour in the Grass*. This discreet shot was nevertheless cut from the American release prints but shown in Europe. Next to breach the line was Carrol Baker in *The Carpetbaggers*. Again the nude scenes were not shown in the United States but included in the European release prints. *Lolita*, the story of a love affair between a thirteen-year-old girl and a middle-aged man, broke through so many previously cherished taboos that the old Code was left in shreds. *Candy* burst through with even more taboo-busting themes of its own, treating sex, and incest, as farce.

Through these breaches, and after a Supreme Court ruling which virtually ended censorship on any grounds, came the pornographers. The hard-core movie, with explicit sexual acts, emerged from the smoky back room into the public cinemas. Although crude and without any redeeming features these movies made many fortunes for the ex-car salesmen who financed them, before organized crime moved in to scoop the pool.

The media started serious speculation on which of the established stars would be the first to appear in an on-screen hard-core sexual act. With European actresses like Brigitte Bardot practically issuing press releases on their sex lives, the betting was on Europe. While simulations moved closer and closer to the real thing none, to this day, has ever reached the public screen, but rumours abound. Instead, to everyone's surprise, the flow moved in the opposite direction. Sylvester Stallone has made no secret of his beginnings in porn movies while Bo Derek actually produced one with her husband John Derek directing. Mrs Derek doesn't appear in the movie but her voice is to be heard speaking for one of the characters. It was all a far cry from the days when Hedy Lamarr and Joan Crawford could spend fortunes buying up copies of their early movies. Crawford would have killed – some hint that she actually did – to protect her secret past. Rumours abound about many other stars who rose from the porno ranks to the more established movie industry and it was to provide a last desperate fall-back for many of the disappointed aspirants that might otherwise have been absorbed into the studio system. The only remnant of the old days was the creak and groan of the couch. There were no long-term contracts any more and so these newcomers – hippies and flower children all – had to work their way from one director to another. The director now became king and, often, the star name of the movies he made.

For a long-term contract the aspirant now turned to the newcomer – television. It was there in the cosiness of the long-running soap that some security could be found. It was to television that the movies ceded the institutionalized couch.

The couch-quickie was now more likely to become a prolonged affair. With their new status directors, especially the newcomers, had more freedom to cast their own discoveries in their pictures – often persevering long past the time when everyone else could see it was a hopeless case. The old lessons, long ago known to Selznick, Goldwyn and Zanuck, had to be learned over again. It has often proved the case that the sparkling personality and ability to express sexuality on screen is usually in inverse proportion to the ability to do the same off screen. It has long been a show business maxim that if you want a truly good performance of, say, a homosexual then you must cast a perfectly straight actor. Many of our sex goddesses were duds in the privacy of their own beds. Which brings us to Marilyn Monroe.

Marilyn's story neatly encapsulates almost every element of the rise and fall of the casting couch. Never was there a more public victim nor a legend of greater endurance. Acres of paper have been covered with stories about her and I would have hesitated to venture further but for a very personal encounter with one of the most central figures in her doomed career – Peter Lawford. I believe he lifted a curtain on the mystery surrounding Marilyn's death which I have not yet seen in print. My contribution to the debate will, I trust, make a fitting end to this account of the casting couch and the virulence of its consequences.

11
The Long Killing of Marilyn

Nobody would be more astonished at the posthumous legendary status accorded Marilyn Monroe than herself, born Norma Jean Mortensen on 1 June 1926, the daughter of an emotionally unstable negative film cutter and a father who had left before Norma Jean was born.

Later in life Marilyn would seek to dramatize her various foster-homes with tales of sexual abuse, rape and abortion but her first husband, Jim Dougherty, has said that she was a virgin on their wedding night in 1942. Pudgy and overweight, she nevertheless delighted both herself and her groom by often greeting him home in the nude and demanding quick sex on the hallway floor. This was a manifestation of her childhood exhibitionist fantasies – when she would dream of stripping off her clothes and have everyone gaze at her in wondrous admiration – and her need to feel wanted. From childhood Marilyn had only felt wanted when praised. She wanted to be a 'good little girl' and all her life sought praise from parental figures. Given her early insecurities this is hardly surprising. The fatal flaw in this developing personality was that her body, and the granting of free use of it, became the only means of self-justification she could rely on.

Briefly employed in an aircraft plant, and with her husband overseas, Marilyn's need for admiration found a receptive outlet when she posed for photographers. Her willingness, in the war years, to spend patient hours posing brought her a great deal of popularity among local professional and amateur photographers. It was one of these who directed a visiting photographer to select her to pose for morale-boosting shots of women in industry. He passed on her name, along with the news that this eighteen-year-old was not averse to ending the session with a little gratification of whatever passions may have been aroused. The high point in her modelling career came when Andre de Dienes not only photographed her but, allegedly, fell in love with her. Marilyn gave thirty-two-year-old de Dienes what she had to offer. He financed her divorce, but their affair ended when he found her in bed with another man.

Marilyn had a compulsive need for affection and no one ever discouraged her from the belief that the only way to return such affection was in bed – whether with men or women.

From the earliest days of her modelling career Marilyn had dreamed of being a movie star. She would latch on to anyone who she thought might be able to influence fate on her behalf. With her detached attitude to sex – most of her lovers report that she was sweet but unresponsive in bed – she was able to view the notorious casting couch with equanimity. Almost all of the photographers that had worked with her reported that at the end of a session it was Marilyn who would look expectantly towards the nearest flat surface.

Ben Lyon, then casting director at Twentieth Century-Fox, was handed some pictures of her, and called her in for an interview. Her responses to his questions were loaded with *doubles entendres*. Marilyn was anxious to show him that she knew the 'score'. Ben Lyon, credited with having discovered Jean Harlow, thought he saw many of the same qualities in Marilyn. He armed her with a letter of introduction and sent her on a round of visits to Twentieth Century executives. Marilyn would bustle smiling into the offices of the gentlemen and hand them the sealed letter of introduction. She was somewhat puzzled when after reading the letter, looking her over and asking a few perfunctory questions they would all do the same thing – walk round their desks with their fly open. It was weeks before Marilyn realized that the letter read: 'This girl really does like giving head.'

Marilyn was to say later that she spent most of her time, in those early days 'on my knees'. Marilyn's labours were not entirely in vain. They brought her a six-month contract at $75 a week. This meant she could attend classes on the Twentieth lot, but also carried the obligation that she make herself 'available' for 'promotional' purposes. Part of this 'obligation' was to attend the night-long poker sessions in company with other contract starlets to act as 'waitresses' and serve the 'boys' drinks and sandwiches as they played through the night. The girls were encouraged to vie with each other to see who could get the most out of a low-cut blouse and the shortest skirts. Opportunities to discuss future career prospects at these get-togethers of Fox executives were limited. The 'boys' made a fetish out of demonstrating machismo. If they wanted a sandwich they would beckon one of the breathlessly waiting girls and point to their plates. If they wanted a drink they would point to their glass. Should they require refreshment of a more intimate nature they would point at their crotch. They had a game at these sessions. It was a point of honour among them to keep a straight face and concentrate on the game in hand rather than show any reaction to the ministrations of the chosen girl kneeling under the table. One night the grand old man of Twentieth Century-Fox – Joe Schenck, nearing seventy years old – was astonished when the chubby blonde he had pointed out went to work with such skill and devotion that she achieved what had become rare for him: a full erection!

Marilyn was moved into a poolhouse at Schenck's house

to be on hand should the body prove willing. The call often came at three in the morning and Marilyn would hurry to perform her specified chore. Being a favourite of one of the founders of Twentieth Century-Fox did nothing for her career prospects. Fox put her into a couple of programmes and then dropped her. Marilyn was indignant. After all, she had performed well for Schenck if not for the movie cameras. Schenck called in a favour from Harry Cohn and Marilyn got a similar 'nothing' contract from Columbia. In 1948, aged twenty-two, she made her one film for Columbia, *Ladies of the Chorus*, in which she had not only some lines but sang two songs – a gift from one of her string of lovers, Fred Karg, head of Columbia's music department. Cohn, on seeing the result, was not pleased. 'What's that fat pig doing in the picture?' he asked, forgetting that he had himself given her the OK after a quickie with her in his office. Marilyn's contract was not renewed despite loyal, and desperate, pleas from Joe Schenck.

During this time of unemployment Marilyn worked variously as a stripper at a place on Sunset Boulevard, as a call girl, and went to bed with almost anyone that she thought might help her. Any newspaperman could count on an interview conducted in various states of undress and, should he actually be able to get something into print, bedroom privileges. Marilyn had little regard for the 'manufactured' image of Marilyn Monroe and constantly thought of herself as Norma Jean who was using this body for career advancement. Norma Jean remained inviolate while men, and women, used Monroe's body.

It was at this time that a highly respected and powerful agent, Johnny Hyde, came into her life. He was fifty-three to her twenty-three, but he did take a serious interest in her career and for the first time there was someone in her bed who could deliver what he promised. Marilyn started getting substantial parts. In 1950 she did small but telling roles in *Asphalt Jungle* and *All About Eve*. Hyde got her a solid contract with Twentieth Century and might have been able to further develop her career except for his weak heart which finally struck him down. Marilyn made one of her many suicide gestures at about this time, but soon recovered enough when she started valuable liaisons with Elia Kazan and, more importantly for her immediate prospects, another ageing Hollywood Mogul, Spyrous Skouras, president of Twentieth Century-Fox. This was fortunate for Marilyn since Darryl Zanuck didn't like her. To please Skouras, however, he upped Marilyn's salary to $450. Marilyn sighed the sigh of many starlets who had slept their way forward. She waved her contract at room-mate Shelley Winters' face and said, 'That's the last cock I'll ever have to suck!' With Shelley Winters, Marilyn had drawn up a list of the ten 'most wanted' men. On it was playwright Arthur Miller. Elia Kazan introduced her to him at the end of 1950. Miller was still married at this time but started a sporadic affair with her. Marilyn was able to triumphantly cross off one name on her list. One of the others was baseball star Joe di Maggio, then newly retired at thirty-seven. To Marilyn, who hardly knew the difference between baseball and football, he was just that – one tick off her list – but to di Maggio she became something of an obsession that was to last after their divorce and her marriage to Arthur Miller.

Meanwhile Zanuck's antipathy was having its effect. Marilyn's career, although now financed by Fox, was stalling. She seemed destined to make nothing but a series of busty walk-ons. She assiduously pursued the Fox publicity men but they took their orders from above and could do nothing that wasn't sanctioned. Marilyn, desperately, embarked on a self-publicizing campaign. Little Norma Jean sent glamorous Marilyn out in gowns slashed to the navel, gave access to anyone with a pen or camera and tried everything, until one day she spotted a nude calendar shot she had posed for in 1949 hanging unremarked on the wall of an office. There was Fox's newest, brightest – in her estimation – starlet hanging completely nude on thousands of walls all over the country and no one knew about it. Marilyn took the story to the Twentieth publicity department. How about creating a news story around this 'scandal'? The studio press department were horrified. They told her it would ruin any career prospects she might have. Marilyn thought differently and 'confidentially' broke the story to two different newspapers. It worked spectacularly. Marilyn became the most talked about starlet in Hollywood and the sales of the calendar shot up and it still sells to this day. Marilyn was launched into *Gentlemen Prefer Blondes* and *How to Marry a Millionaire*. Marilyn was, finally, a fully fledged movie star. To Fox's amazement they found that Marilyn's sad little explanation – 'I was broke at the time and needed the money to pay my rent' – endeared her to men and women all over America. For Marilyn it was the beginning of a series of pathos-based fictions about her early life in which her parents were dead (her mother was, in fact, in a mental institution); her father was a farmer in the Midwest, or living in California or – the one story that nobody printed – that she was the result of a liaison between her mother and Clark Gable.

About this time she started attending the kinky sex parties organized by Peter Lawford. Lawford was related to the Kennedys by marriage, and his place was considered a safe one for the star names of the day to let it all hang out. Marilyn was a star of many of Lawford's little gatherings which also featured the famed Hollywood Rat Pack led by Frank Sinatra.

Marilyn revelled in the company of strong, secure and,

preferably, older men. They gave her the confidence she so badly lacked. Their estimation of her as a 'piece of meat' suitable for occasional usage became her own. The public, rapidly raising her to sex goddess status, terrified her. Acting terrified her. Norma Jean did her best to keep pace with Marilyn but it was a losing battle from the start.

She needed reassurance on the tiniest little detail of her life. After a night with Marlon Brando she worried for weeks that she 'hadn't done "it" right'. She would summon people from half way across town because she couldn't decide which dress to wear. She would allow others to spend hours on her hair and make-up and then destroy all their efforts by 'remembering' that she had yet to shower and so undo all that had been done. Anything to delay having to face the world as Marilyn Monroe.

She tried shielding behind marriages with di Maggio (1954) and Arthur Miller (1956), but they couldn't prevent the living nightmares she suffered. She became afraid to live, afraid to sleep, afraid to wake. An endless routine of barbiturates and alcohol did nothing but confuse her further.

In 1956, two weeks after marrying Miller, Marilyn went to England to make *The Prince and the Showgirl* with Laurence Olivier.

After reports of the trauma Olivier and everyone else suffered during the making of this so-so success, Marilyn wasn't to work again for nearly two years. During this time she tried to fulfil her lifelong wish to become a mother. All attempts ended in a series of miscarriages for which she blamed herself and the abortions – nine to twelve – which she had undergone in her pre-pill starlet days.

Marilyn resumed her career with a courageous Billy Wilder in *Some Like it Hot*. Her lateness and unreliability nearly destroyed both director and co-stars, Jack Lemmon and Tony Curtis. Only the box office smash success of the movie saved Marilyn's career. George Cukor bravely took her on for a movie project called *Let's Make Love*. His problem was that none of the established Hollywood leading men of the day wanted to do it with Marilyn. Yul Brynner, Rock Hudson and Gregory Peck were among those who declined. Desperate, Cukor turned to French song and dance actor Yves Montand, with whom Marilyn immediately started an affair, much to the chagrin of Montand's wife, actress Simone Signoret. Marilyn wanted marriage, Montand was content with the wife he had. After this episode Marilyn went to pieces. Her promiscuity took on the desperation of someone wanting to prove that she was still attractive to men. She would invite almost anyone that showed the slightest response into bed. Through the following months this included delivery boys, men working on her newly acquired house, and bartenders in addition to the stars she met and mated at Peter Lawford's parties. One recipient of her favours at this time was a personal friend of mine who reported that the experience was 'unreal'. She had come up to him at a party and insisted that they had met before in London. Finally they ended up coupling standing up in the kitchen of the house, with the Mexican help looking on in wide-eyed wonder. Throughout the episode Marilyn kept breathily telling him that he 'was fucking Marilyn Monroe' as if she were talking about a third party and urging him to 'give the bitch what she deserves'. Afterwards, he reports, Marilyn clung to him and wanted to slip out the back door with him and for him to drive her home. Suddenly he realized that she was extremely drunk, but before he could do anything two men, one dressed like a chauffeur, the other a mean-looking 'Mafia' type, grabbed her away from him. One hustled Marilyn out of the house while the other stayed long enough to issue a chilling warning. My friend didn't know who either of these men were, or their connection with Marilyn – and, wisely, didn't ask.

Within a year of this episode Marilyn was dead. Almost everyone – and that's everyone! – that has ever written about Marilyn's last days has concentrated their energies on that last weekend, 4 and 5 August 1962. The result has been confusion, with speculations ranging from questions about whether or not she died in the ambulance rushing her to hospital after a self-administered overdose, or if she was given a lethal injection in that ambulance and returned to her house to die in her own bed. Was the emergency call to the police delayed so that Bobby Kennedy could make good his escape? Everyone from the Mafia to the FBI and the CIA has been implicated in one way or another. The truth has been confused and distorted simply because everyone has been looking in the wrong place and at the wrong weekend.

What happened that earlier weekend is a nightmare – so awful and horrific that much time and money was spent by famous and powerful men to conceal it and confuse later investigators.

My inkling into what really happened came over a lunch with one of the leading players in the drama – Peter Lawford.

In May 1984 I was in Hollywood to set up a comedy-caper movie with a producer who was being primarily financed by an Italian company. One morning we got a call from our Italian financiers asking us to make contact with Peter Lawford who they wanted for a cameo part in another movie they then had in production. They were prepared to offer him very little money and we had no copy of the script which neither of us had even read. Nevertheless we set about trying to trace him.

Peter Lawford hadn't worked in a very long time. Word

was that his former friends and associates were shunning him and that he was 'locked out' of the major studios. Finding him therefore presented some major difficulties. None of the more prestigious agencies which would have once been pleased to handle him now even knew his number or where he could be reached. We eventually traced him to an apartment in West Hollywood and, without enthusiasm, called him up. Lawford, as expected, didn't respond to our vague proposition and the contact, apparently, fizzled out. Later, to our surprise, he called back and we set up a meeting for lunch the following day.

My companion and I discussed how best to approach him over the lunch. We were both painfully aware that the Italians were merely seeking to exploit the tatters of a past reputation which they saw as getting a 'name' on the cheap. We decided to sweeten the offer by employing the old Hollywood ploy of holding out a promise of something better in the future. We had with us a screenplay called *Bloody Mary* in which there was a central role for an ageing playboy and, in the absence of a script of the role he was really wanted for, decided to concentrate on this.

Lawford appeared for lunch looking like a travesty of his former self. It was obvious he was seriously ill, and we felt even more guilty as we outlined the original proposal to him. He listened politely enough but then turned down the 'offer' cold. Much as he would enjoy the expenses-paid trip to Europe he still wanted more money than was being currently offered. We then brought the *Bloody Mary* ploy into play.

'What's that about?' he asked.

I outlined the story of a woman's revenge on the powerful man who had wronged her. It was a story much in vogue at the time.

'What did they do to her?' Lawford asked, apparently interested.

'She had an affair with this rich, powerful man and then he ditched her. After being ditched she finds out she's pregnant. She calls him up and threatens to expose him, using the blood test on the baby, when born, to prove her story. He responds by having her abducted and forcibly aborted, so destroying the "evidence".'

Lawford looked as if he had been struck by lightning. He stared at me for what seemed minutes before he started shaking visibly. He rose to his feet, still staring at me with what I thought was some insanity. 'Are you crazy?' he yelled at me, attracting the attention of all the other diners. 'You want to get us all fucking killed?' With that he rushed off the restaurant terrace leaving myself and my colleague to wonder what it was we'd said. We didn't reach any conclusion and reported back that Lawford wasn't interested and, in any case, neither mentally nor physically fit to work.

A year later I was watching a documentary on Marilyn when the memory of Lawford's mysterious reaction on the restaurant terrace came back to me and I finally understood.

There is much published evidence of Marilyn's sexual encounters with John F Kennedy and his younger brother Robert. In pursuing Hollywood starlets and stars they were following in the family tradition set by Joseph Kennedy, who conducted many Hollywood affairs including one with Gloria Swanson. Marilyn was mesmerized throughout her life by men who she thought were positive achievers. Despite her many experiences of being used she was still capable of thinking of every man she went to bed with as having a long-term romantic relationship in mind. During her affair with the president she seriously thought of herself as a potential first lady. Even when he passed the potentially explosive time bomb that Marilyn had become down to his younger brother, Marilyn's delusions remained intact. Now it was Robert Kennedy that was going to marry her.

Shortly before making *Something's Got to Give*, which was finally abandoned, Marilyn found she was, once again, pregnant. At thirty-six time was fast running out for her to be a mother. Countless abortions and miscarriages had failed to dim the light that burned somewhere in the back of her confused mind. Certain that the father was Robert Kennedy and deluded by his pillow talk into believing that he would marry her, Marilyn further convinced herself that a baby was all they needed to bring them together.

How anyone, with even the most fevered of self-deluding minds, could imagine that the second most prominent Catholic politician in America could divorce his wife and leave his children to set up house with an already pregnant sex symbol is beyond most people's understanding, but Marilyn believed it. She spoke to many people about the 'man in politics' who was going to divorce his wife and marry her.

When her attempts to call Robert on his private line and share the good news failed she was sure there was some misunderstanding. She tried placing calls through the Justice Department's switchboard and again met with a stone wall. What she didn't know was that John F Kennedy had warned his brother of the potentially explosive situation building up and advised him to cut Marilyn off. If America's Number One sex symbol were to produce a baby which was proven to be Bobby's then all hell would break loose and the Kennedy dynasty would be threatened.

It was at this point that Marilyn became dispensable. To anyone outside the rarefied heights of high-level politics or, to a lesser extent, the movie industry, it would seem unbelievable that rational men could come to a decision to force the termination of Monroe's baby. To understand that you have to place yourself inside the cocoon of self-importance and genuine power wielded by these men and then look out at the manufactured blonde bimbo who threatens it all. To men who could order the assassination of Heads of State for reasons of political convenience the spectre of a practically friendless glamour girl would seem to be nothing at all.

To the public Marilyn was, and still is, an unattainable remote goddess. To the men called in to discuss what 'had' to be done she was an all-too-obtainable piece of entertainment who had spent three-quarters of her life being 'agreeable' to all and sundry. Somewhere along the line she'd got lucky but now was looking dangerous.

The man elected to approach Marilyn and tell her what had to be done – abortion was almost a routine with her, having clocked up around thirteen at this time in her life – and add a mixture of threats and promises was Peter Lawford. Marilyn was horrified. She was convinced that Lawford was acting in his own interests and without the knowledge of the Kennedys. All Lawford's talk did was to cause her to redouble her efforts to reach Bobby Kennedy. When she failed she turned back to Peter Lawford because he was the only channel open to her. He promised her a face-to-face meeting with both the Kennedys. This came down to arranging for her to interrupt shooting on *Something's Got to Give* to fly to Washington to sing 'Happy Birthday' to John Kennedy at a public function.

Marilyn was sewn into a gown which was little more than a sheen of sequins on her naked body. She, high on pills, booze and expectations, crooned the simple ditty as if she were putting over a smutty song in a night club.

In response to this ill-judged display the President rose to say: 'Now I can retire from politics after having "Happy

Birthday" sung to me in such a "sweet", "wholesome" way!' The irony of his words, knowing what he did of Marilyn's condition and the circumstances haunting both him and the Attorney General, were completely lost on Marilyn. She flew back to Hollywood in the highest of spirits and – unusually – reported back for work at Twentieth Century prompt to time!

Marilyn was in high spirits throughout that week. Scheduled to do a now famous scene in a flesh-coloured bikini she decided to 'knock their eyes out' and reported on set for her scheduled swim completely nude. The nude shots the assigned studio photographers took that day were to net them something close to a quarter of a million dollars in syndicated rights. It is ironic to note that Marilyn was being paid only $100,000 for the entire movie.

This is no criticism of the photographers involved. They, ethically, showed the pictures to Marilyn before release. Marilyn gave them her blessing with the words, 'That should knock Liz Taylor off the front pages for once!'

It also gave harassed producer Henry Weinstein some relief from the stop-start progress of the movie. That week things went smoothly. He would have rested less easily had he known the bomb that was to go off that weekend of 2 and 3 June.

On Friday 1 June 1962 the technical crew of *Something's Got to Give* threw an on-set birthday party for Marilyn. She was thirty-six years old. The cake, ordered before she decided to swim nude, showed her reclining in a bikini. She was happy and relaxed and she chatted and kissed cheeks with all and sundry. That same night, looking more happy and radiant than she had in a long time, she threw out the first ball in a baseball game. That was the eve of Marilyn's 'lost weekend'.

Henry Weinstein was quoted as later saying, 'Something happened that weekend. Nobody knows what. I mean, people *do* know, but nobody's saying.'

Later that month Marilyn was to tell a woman journalist: 'A woman has to love a man with all her heart when she has his child when they're not married. And when a man leaves a woman, when she tells him she's going to have his baby – when he doesn't marry her, that must hurt a woman very much. Deep down inside.'

To hairdresser Agnes Flanagan, Marilyn broke down. She told Agnes that she was 'looking so poorly' because she'd just had an abortion in Mexico.

To long-time friend Arthur James she said she'd 'just lost a baby'.

Jose Bolanos, a Mexican writer with whom Marilyn had had an affair, was to say, after Marilyn's death, that she telephoned him and told him 'something' that 'will one day shake the world'. Whatever that was he has yet to share it.

Abortion was illegal in the California of 1962. The answer was to take a trip to Mexico and that is where Marilyn would have had to go if she had *voluntarily* wanted an abortion.

The question is, why would she? The biological clock was running out on her hopes of ever being a mother, something she had longed for all her life. She was midway through a come-back picture which was going well. She well knew, from her previous dozen or so experiences, that an abortion would make it impossible for her to work the following week and the resultant publicity would not only end her hopes of a baby but her career as well.

It is, then, extremely unlikely that Marilyn went voluntarily to Mexico. What is the alternative? I believe that Peter Lawford's outburst on hearing the scenario I outlined to him, and the obvious fear that drove him from people offering him badly needed work, supplies a reasonable alternative which explains both Marilyn's abortion that weekend and her despair and subsequent actions. I firmly believe that, during the early hours of Saturday 1 June 1962, Marilyn was taken forcibly from her home, and flown to Mexico for an abortion she didn't want to have.

If so it was one of the most infamous outrages ever committed on a woman's body. Rape victims suffer trauma; imagine the effect of having a much-wanted baby killed against your wishes. Such an event would have destroyed many much stronger personalities than Marilyn's. To her it would have been the apocalyptic climax to a lifetime of submitting her body to others' demands. There would have been a void in both body and spirit.

Everyone connected with Marilyn agrees that in the week following her 'lost weekend' Marilyn was changed. Pale, drawn, almost incapable of getting out of bed or leaving her house, she sought help.

In the early hours of Monday morning Marilyn called her psychiatrist, Dr Greenson. He was away in Europe but his son and daughter were so concerned at Marilyn's distress that they decided to go in his stead. They found Marilyn heavily drugged, depressed and rambling. They called in a colleague of Dr Greenson's. He took away her armoury of drugs but decided there was little else he could do.

The studio is told that Marilyn is too sick to work. They wait out her recovery until 20 June, when they formally dismiss her from the picture.

Marilyn now swings from moods of black depression to something approaching euphoria. Giving an interview in a restaurant she claims her body never looked better and, in public, pulls up her sweater to expose her bra-less breasts to prove it. For *Vogue* she unexpectedly insists on posing nude. Her exhibitionism, always present, took on new dimensions as if she were desperately trying to prove that she still *had* a body. The spirit was broken.

At the end of July she took a trip to Lake Tahoe in the company of the ubiquitous Peter Lawford and his Kennedy wife, Pat. Why did she go? She had earlier told her physician, Dr Firestone, that she 'was being pressured to go to parties' and that 'she didn't like Peter Lawford because he was always having big orgies'.

Di Maggio, desperate to help her, and knowing the nature of the parties she was attending, tried to stop her. Later he was to tell Harry Hall, 'She went up there. They gave her pills. They had sex parties.'

Frank Sinatra, newly returned from Monte Carlo, took pictures that weekend of Marilyn which, after her death, he burned. Those pictures of a drugged, spaced-out Marilyn might, in other hands, have been used as highly effective 'evidence' of her moral and mental condition should she have considered going public on what had happened to her and who had been involved. It might well be that Peter Lawford assembled his cast of perverts for just such a purpose. Whatever it was that induced Marilyn to attend this particular, hated, orgy, it was to be her last.

Marilyn returned to Los Angeles after that Lake Tahoe weekend aboard Sinatra's private plane. She was accompanied by Peter Lawford, who according to the pilot, was as drunk as she was. He later told his wife, 'She was out of it. A mess.' Marilyn herself spoke of that weekend as 'A nightmare, really dreadful.'

The following Saturday night Marilyn was to die. Whoever was there or not there, whether or not they gave her a lethal injection or whether she took the barbiturate herself is all, in the light of the above, irrelevant. They had killed off Marilyn Monroe six weeks earlier. It just took a little while for everyone around her to notice.

It is obvious that no one connected with such a series of horrific events would come forward and admit to having taken part, but I believe that Peter Lawford inadvertently supplied the missing link. Here was a man who had been at the very epicentre of all that happened in the Kennedy world for years. A man, once of influence and social standing, now shunned, ruined and living on the charity of others. Desperately in need of a paying job and self-respect he ran when confronted with a storyline. That storyline was based on a British divorce case, but obviously Lawford thought he was being set up and that I knew more than I pretended.

Lawford would have been the obvious choice to set up something like this cruel and cynical operation. Had that baby been born the fear for the Kennedys would have been that Marilyn might have been able to prove her story about the father's identity. Even if she hadn't been able to prove it, in the legal sense, the resulting publicity would have been the end of the Kennedys' political dynasty. Without the baby it was simply Marilyn's word against theirs – Marilyn's word, spattered and besmirched by photographs showing her in the company of several men performing sexual acts which would have been repugnant to public feeling. Marilyn would have had no chance against the two most powerful men in America.

Only Peter Lawford's blandishments and promises of a meeting with Robert Kennedy held Marilyn in check during those last weeks of her life. That fatal last Saturday Marilyn had her last meeting with Robert Kennedy at her home. There, unknown to either, their last, noisy confrontation was recorded by a clandestine tape recorder. The tapes of that last meeting were known about and played by a very few insiders. They were explosive evidence against the then Attorney General. By some means or other Robert Kennedy was confronted with this irrefutable evidence and managed to acquire it. From then on the tapes ceased to exist.

Peter Lawford would have known the truth which vast resources were deployed to hide. I believe he revealed that truth when he rushed ashen-faced and visibly shaking from that restaurant in May 1984. What else would have caused a man so desperately seeking self-respect to run from an offer crying: 'You want to get us all fucking killed?'

12
A Parade Gone By

The sixties saw the end of the old Hollywood which has been the subject of this book. Career advancement in exchange for sexual favours was never quite unique to Hollywood and, of itself, has not ended. What has passed is the Studio System, the Moguls that shaped it in their own image, and the frame in which raw beauty could be invested with star quality. Louis B Mayer spent four years and untold dollars on shaping a bare-foot southern girl with an accent that was almost incomprehensible into the very lovely ultra-sophisticate they named Ava Gardner. In this day of independent production there is neither the time nor the money to make such long-term, high-risk investments. Today any aspiring star has to work piece-meal from picture to picture, putting their own money into training classes and press agents.

Part of the initial process of star building was inevitably the casting couch. While it was cynical, cruel, callous and humiliating it was as much used by its 'victims' as abused by those in a position to impose it.

For those who sentimentalize about its victims it may be salutary to remind them that Marilyn Monroe would, without it, today be just another overweight waitress in a fast-food outlet. Those the Studio System sought to destroy it had first to create.

The Moguls who founded and controlled the industry throughout what are now recalled as the Golden Years forged the system on their knowledge of the streets and ghettoes from which they, for the most part, came. They flew by the seats of their pants or, as Harry Cohn once put it, 'by the itch of my ass'. They knew little about cost accounting or cash flow charts. All they knew was what the public would buy. Today Hollywood is governed by graduates of law schools and accountants who have lived their lives cocooned in comfortable middle-class structured lives. All they know of real people is contained in statistics. The old-time Moguls made movies – their successors make deals. Movie-making is left to those eccentric creative people who have somehow acquired the magical ability to tell a lens from a lease-back.

Zanuck, Cohn, Mayer and Selznick would have been appalled at what has happened to the empires they founded. Today's coke-fuelled movie executives treat the 'old-timers' with contempt while regressing the American movie industry into the realm of comic book romps. The old system produced crass commercial pictures in a ratio of a hundred to one against really good worthwhile movies but they did, at least, make more of them and no one postured pretentiously over a rewrite of a fairy tale set in space as if it were some great creative achievement. They knew their business because it *was* their business. As a corollary came the Moguls' despotism and megalomania. To their famous contract artists in their Beverly Hills homes the Moguls became 'monsters', 'ogres' and all the other epithets at their command. Today these 'ogres' have gone the way of the dinosaur and there are many who mourn the possibility of the structured career that went with them.

The casting couch was shipped out of the movie studios and ceded to the makers of television series where the spirit of the old Moguls still lives. Even there they demand their talent comes pre-packaged and ready to use. The luxurious four years of expenses-paid training enjoyed by Ava Gardner and thousands like her that never made it is very much a thing of the past except in one tiny area.

The new kings of Hollywood are no longer the producers but the directors. They are the charismatic names to which the public responds. This new generation of directors have, in many cases, become their own 'star' names, and find themselves selling more readily than the very expensive and very few bankable actor names available to them. This has led many of them to keep alive the old Moguls' dream of finding a raw talent and developing its star quality. Not having the old studios' resources their efforts are necessarily confined to one girl at a time, but the delusion is as strong in them as it ever was when Goldwyn scoured Europe in the twenties for 'his' star, or Zanuck pursued the same dream across a half-dozen affairs in the fifties.

These affairs cannot be classified under the same heading as the casting-couch quickie since the participants are able to delude themselves that theirs is an affair of the heart as much as a career move.

Since all directors today share this same dream it is, perhaps, unfair to single out any one of them, but Peter Bogdanovich has selected himself.

Bogdanovich's first essay into star-making was with Cybil Shepherd, with whom he persisted through four movies before realizing that the public wasn't buying. Cybil's career was resuscitated by the success of the TV series *Moonlighting* but Bogdanovich's search went on.

He next lighted on Dorothy Stratton who, in 1979, had just been selected Playmate of the Year. Dorothy had first come to Hollywood at eighteen in the company of her husband, Paul Snider. The connection with Hugh Hefner and the publicity she got earned her a couple of unremarkable movie roles before she met Bogdanovich. He became certain she had, at twenty, 'star quality' and in furtherance of his aims had her move in with him to tutor her more closely. The resentment that this caused in

Dorothy's husband, Snider, seems to have taken Hollywood by surprise. Being an 'outsider' he obviously didn't understand the rules! Hollywood accused him of trying to 'cash in on Dorothy's fame', overlooking the inconvenient fact that that was exactly what they were trying to do. Snider's crime, apparently, was that he found Dorothy working behind a shop counter and promoted her modelling career to the ultimate in the model's dream, Playmate of the Year. At this point, and given Bogdanovich's interest, it seemed to Hollywood only natural that Snider should fade quietly away and leave it to the 'professionals' – i.e. those who had exploited more than one girl before. They characterized Snider as a 'cheap crook' trying to 'muscle in'.

Dorothy knew that her best chances lay with Bogdanovich and wanted to stay where she was. Snider took further exception and blasted her – and himself – to death with a shotgun. Hollywood doesn't seem to realize that this hardly squares with a man who was out simply to exploit Dorothy. If that had been the case then he would have realized that he would stand to gain more by 'selling' her by way of settlement than killing her. Meanwhile the men who contemptuously dismiss Snider as an exploiter forget that he also showed the passion to marry the girl and then the jealousy to kill both her and himself.

Bogdanovich's obsession with Dorothy didn't end with her death. When Dorothy died, aged twenty, she left behind her mother and a twelve-year-old sister, Louise. It was to them that Bogdanovich turned his attentions. At the time of writing Louise, now twenty, has just married Bogdanovich, having undergone extensive plastic surgery to increase her resemblance to the dead Dorothy. Whether or not Bogdanovich intends to pursue his dream of creating a new star out of the Stratton family remains to be seen. It is entirely possible he will run into the same roadblock which has plagued all such previous attempts to 'make' a star.

The question that arises is whether the entire star system – a fervent belief in Hollywood since Florence Lawrence first burst into public notice – is not simply a delusion.

The public, first and foremost, go to see a *movie*. Where the 'star' name delusion first got its airing was that a particular actor or actress became identified with a certain kind of movie which labelled it as the *kind of movie* they wanted to see that particular night. The Moguls knew this. They kept their stars playing the same movie over and over again. The public could be absolutely sure of what they were buying when they went to see an Errol Flynn or a Betty Grable or a Doris Day. Monroe would always be a sympathetic floozie on the make, and Cary Grant would always be a rich smoothie. If the public were flocking to their movies because they *labelled* it rather than simply because they were *in* it, then Hollywood has been expending millions of dollars over eighty years for not much return. The test of this came when the actors stepped outside their expected roles. Most of them, with honourable exceptions, crashed to oblivion. Currently Sylvester Stallone and Clint Eastwood can be relied on to draw audiences. Is there anyone out there that doesn't have an instant insight into what *kind* of movie they are going to be in? What price Bo Derek as a downtrodden housewife (or, come to that, given all the hype at the time of *10*, anything)? Barbra Streisand tried that in *All Through the Night* and nobody came because it wasn't *Funny Girl*. If there is any validity in the star name theory, why not? The public flock to a James Bond movie no matter who plays him. The actors that really break through are those that stick with an established image. Those that complain about being typecast and try to break away and create a new image usually find themselves heading for oblivion. They don't realize that their fame was due to the type of movie they were in, not themselves. The Moguls knew that and half their problems came from actors that didn't. They held the old Hollywood together and without them Hollywood has become diffuse to the point where the most commonly heard cry is: 'Nobody knows anymore!' Wouldn't it be sweet irony if the cause of their confusion was that they had missed the point?

Epilogue

One lady that spoke candidly and openly about the casting couch never did become an international star but had a good career. She took time out for two marriages, one to a cameraman and the second to a businessman who died leaving her independently wealthy. Lately she's returned to the business and currently is enjoying a featured role in a prime-time soap. Her words speak for the thousands that experienced the casting couch.

'What you have to understand about the girls that came to Hollywood is that, back then, in the late forties, it was the end of the road.

'I came out of a small town. Ever since I'd become a woman people had been telling me that I "ought to be in movies". Eventually, with money given me by my mother, I came west. It was like running away to a circus. There was nothing out there that had any resemblance to the life I'd left behind me. Nothing. Not the way they spoke, dressed or behaved.

'Suddenly I wasn't the Belle of the Ball any more. I was one among thousands and all the girls looked twice as beautiful and twice as sophisticated, and knew ten times more than I did. I was just the newest clown on the block.

'Now this casting couch thing. Do you have any idea how sexually attractive those men were to us? Forget what they looked like. Listen, there's no more powerful aphrodisiac in the world than a man with power. Especially when it's the power to make your dreams come true. I don't think many girls were dragged kicking and screaming to bed!

'After some of the phony characters – the exploiters – that I and every other girl I knew came into contact with in those first few months, meeting Harry Cohn – he was older than my father – and having him "take an interest" in me was like having a personal interview with an oriental potentate.

'Harry Cohn treated me like a hooker and, in a way, I deserved nothing more. The thing is that, in his presence, I didn't care. I absolutely thought that my "thing" with him was the most exciting thing that had ever happened to me. I truly did. I didn't feel ashamed of it. In fact I went around telling all my girlfriends, in precise detail, what had happened – and they were *jealous*!

'I'll tell you something else. Cohn kept his promises to me. He put me under contract and he would often see me passing in the studio – he kept an eye on everybody coming and going – and he would nod and smile.

'I know for a fact he put me into parts where I wasn't particularly wanted. Harry Cohn was a foul-mouthed sadistic bully but he would only have to snap his fingers and I'd come running. [Peals of laughter from interviewee] . . . and you can interpret that any way you like!

'No, anyone that tells you that we girls were some kind of victims is not telling the whole truth. There was a world of lights, glamour, riches and fame out there and these men had the power to give you all that. There's many a girl gone to bed for less.

'I know that after Harry Cohn screwed me I had status. I felt like Miss America – as if I'd won some kind of national contest. In a way I had.'

Index

Index

Affectionately Yours 149
Aker, Jean 56–7
Alamo, The 180–82
Albin, Charles 106
All About Eve 198
All Through the Night 217
Anastasia 136
Angeli, Pier 175–6
Angry Silence, The 176
Arbuckle, Fatty 52–5, 70
Arthur, Jean 118
Asphalt Jungle 198
Astor, Mary 105–8
Atwill, Lionel 98, 101, 137, 138–9

Baker Carrol 191
Bankhead, Tallulah 114–15
Bara, Theda 30–31
Barbarian and the Geisha, The 179
Bardot, Brigitte 191
Barry, Joan 145–7
Barrymore, John 106–7, 115
Beau Brummel 107
Beaumont, Harry 79
Beery, Wallace 98–9
Belafonte, Harry 168
Bell, Rex 60, 62
Belle of the Nineties 141
Belle Starr 153
Ben Hur 96
Bergman, Ingrid 134–6, 163
Berkeley, Busby 95, 96, 109
Bern, Paul 87–92
Beyond The Rainbow 57
Birth of a Nation 31, 96
Black Pirate, The 154
Blonde Bombshell 91

Blood and Sand 149
Blue Angel, The 99–100
Blythe, Betty 96
Bogdanovich, Peter 215–16
Bogart, Humphrey 182
Boggs, Francis 24
Bolanos, Jose 208
Bonjour Tristesse 178
Bout de Souffle, A 178
Bow, Clara 57–62, 69, 79, 84–5
Brando, Marlon 200
Bright Road 168–9
Brody, Sam 174
Brooks, Louise 49–52
Brown, Kay 120, 162
Brunner, Yul 201
Bus Stop 172

Cabot, Bruce 140
Candy 191
Cansino, Eduardo 147
Cantor, Eddie 58, 126
Caprice, June 95
Captain Blood 117
Carmen Jones 168–9
Carpetbaggers, The 191
Cassini, Oleg 153
Casting Couch, The 13–14, 75, 76, 77
Chandler, Jeff 177
Chaplin, Charles 15, 21, 22, 26, 33–5, 63–9, 118, 143–7
Chaplin, Sydney 63–4, 124–5
Charge of the Light Brigade, The 117
Chatterton, Ruth 27
Citizen Kane 150
Claudia 162

Clifton, Elmer 57
Cohn, Harry 48, 79–80, 133, 149–50, 152, 176–7, 182, 197, 213–14, 220
Colbert, Claudette 96, 100
Coming Home 76
Conklin, Chester 29
Cooper, Gary 59, 182
Costello, Dolores 125
Count of Monte Cristo, The 24
Crawford, Joan 14, 27, 72–81, 192
Crosby, Bing 176
Cukor, George 115, 116, 117, 120, 201
Cummings Irving 153
Curtis, Tony 201

Damita, Lila 100
Damone, Vic 175–6
Dancing Daughters 79
Dandridge, Dorothy 168–70
Daniels, Bebe 27
Darnell, Linda 103–4, 163
Darvi, Bella 182–9
Davies, Marion 36–8, 67–8
Davis, Bette 27, 157–8
Davis, Sammy, Jnr 177–8
Day, Doris 217
Day at the Races, A 168
Daytime Wife 104
Dean, James 175
Decks Ran Red, The 170
de Dienes, Andre 195
de Havilland, Olivia 27, 81, 117
Delmont, Maude 53, 54
de Mille, Cecil B 96, 108, 144–5, 182
Derek, Bo 192, 217
Derek, John 192
Devil is a Woman, The 100
Devoe, Daisy 60–62
Dial M for Murder 176
Diary of a Lost Girl 51
Dickson, Joan 160
Dietrich, Marlene 99–101, 134

di Maggio, Joe 198, 200, 210
Dishonoured 100
Dixey, Phyllis 20–21
Dodge City 117
Domergue, Faith 160
Dove, Billie 154
Down to the Sea in Ships 58
Dozier, Bill 79–80

East of Eden 175
Eastwood, Clint 217
Ecstasy 95
Edison, Thomas 23
Ekberg, Anita 191
Entwhistle, Peg 97–8
Essanay 23
Ethridge, La Jeanne 180–81

Fairbanks, Douglas 109
Farewell to Arms, A 165
Faye, Alice 109
Feldman, Charles 94
Flanagan, Agnes 208
Fleming, Victor 59
Flynn, Errol 102, 117, 118, 139–40, 182, 217
Fonda, Henry 133, 153
Fontaine, Joan 27, 117, 157
Fool There Was, A 31
Ford, Glenn 150
Ford, John 153
Four From Texas 191
Fox, Virginia 124, 125, 127, 186–7
Fox, William 182
Francis, Kay 27
Franken, Rose 162
From Here To Eternity 80, 167
Front Page, The 155
Funny Girl 217

Gable, Clark 114, 132, 133, 199
Garbo, Greta 133–5
Gardner, Ava 157, 213, 214
Garland, Judy 92–3
Gary, Romain 178, 179

Gaucho 109
Geisler, Jerry 140
Gentlemen Prefer Blondes 199
Gentlemen's Agreement 131, 168
Gilda 150
Gilles, Genevieve 189
Girl Can't Help It, The 172
Gish, Dorothy 27, 28, 32, 56
Gish, Lilian 27–8, 32, 106
Goddard, Paulette 27, 118, 143–5
Gold Rush, The 65
Goldwyn, Samuel 82, 159, 193, 215
Gone to Earth 165
Gone with the Wind 46, 114, 117, 144
Grable, Betty 96–7, 128, 130, 217
Granger, Stewart 160–61
Grant, Cary 162, 217
Granville, Bonita 92
Grapes of Wrath, The 168
Greer, Jane 159–60
Grey, Lita 34, 35, 64–7, 69
Griffith, D. W. 31–2, 106

Hansen, Betty 139–40
Hansen, Juanita 30, 71
Harlow, Jean 27, 84–92, 155
Harriet Craig 79
Harris, Mildred 34–5, 64, 66
Harrison, Rex 109
Hathaway, Henry 153
Having a Wonderful Time 112–13
Hayden, Sterling 80
Hays, William 71
Hayward, Susan 120
Hayworth, Rita 147–52, 176
Hearst, William Randolph 36–8, 67–9, 182
Heart of a Race Riot 24
Hedren, Tippi 176–7
Hell's Angels 84, 86, 155
Hepburn, Katherine 155
Hitchcock, Alfred 164, 176–7
Honeymoon, The 32
Hoover, J. Edgar 178

Hopkins, Miriam 27, 116, 153
Hopper, Hedda 62
Horne, Lena 168
Howard, Jean 93–4
Howard, Leslie 102, 134
Howard, Trevor 170
How to Marry a Millionaire 199
Hudson, Rock 201
Hughes, Howard 84, 85–6, 105, 117, 118, 153–61, 171–5
Hush, Hush, Sweet Charlotte 81
Huston, John 117, 179–80
Hutton, Betty 27
Hyde, Johnny 197–8

I, Claudius 102
Ince, Thomas 68
Indiscreet 136
Inn of the Sixth Happiness, The 136
Intolerance 31, 96

James, Arthur 208
Janis, Elsie 40–43
Jeanne Engels 177
Jessel, George 126
Jet Pilot 174
Johnny Guitar 80
Jolson, Al 126
Jones, Jennifer 162–4, 165
Judson, Edward 148, 150
Jurgens, Curt 170
Justin, John 169–70

Kalem 23
Karg, Fred 197
Karno, Fred 15, 17–21, 33
Kazan, Elia 191, 198
Kellerman, Annette 31, 95
Kelly, Grace 176
Kennedy, John F 204, 205, 206–7
Kennedy, Joseph 204
Kennedy, Robert 204–6, 211–12
Kerr, Deborah 80
Keyes, Evelyn 116–17
Khan, Prince Aly 151, 152, 153

King of Kings 96
Kiss Them For Me 172
Korda, Alexander 102

Ladies of the Chorus 197
Laemmle, Carl 25–6, 39
Lake, Veronica 157
LaMarr, Barbara 56, 69, 71, 95
Lamarr, Hedy 69–70, 95, 192
Landis, Carole 108, 128, 149
Lang, Fritz 153
Lasky, Jesse 182
Laughton, Charles 101
Laurel, Stan 15, 21, 22, 29
Lawford, Peter 170, 199, 201–12
Lawrence, Florence 25–6, 217
Lee, Gypsy Rose 20
Leigh, Janet 174
Leigh, Vivien 120
Lemmon, Jack 200
Let's Make Love 201
Light Touch, The 175
Lindstrom, Per 136
Litvak, Anatole 153
Lock, John 50
Lolita 191
Lombard, Carole 27, 133
Lopez, Virginia 137–9
Love, Bessie 13, 32
Loy, Myrna 27
Lubin 23
Lubitsch, Ernst 140–42
Lugosi, Bela 59
Lyon, Ben 195

Malaga 170
Malcolm X 178
Manners, Elsie 19–20, 21, 22
Mansfield, Jayne 171–4
Mantrap 58
Man with the Golden Arm, The 167, 177
Marley, Peverell 104
Mature, Victor 132, 150
Maxwell, Elsa 152
Mayer, Louis B 34–5, 48, 76, 78, 86, 87, 89–90, 92–5, 163, 182, 213, 214
MacArthur, Douglas 137
McMurray, Nana 64, 65, 66, 67
Melies 23
Merry Widow, The 32
Miller, Arthur 198, 200
Millette, Dorothy 88–9, 91
Minter, Mary Miles 55–6, 70, 90, 108
Modern Times 143
Monroe, Marilyn 27, 172, 173, 174, 193–211
Montand, Yves 201
Montgomery, Robert 132
Moon is Blue, The 167
Moonlighting 215
Moore, Colleen 56
Moore, Owen 40
Morocco 100
Morrison, Charles 120
Morrison, Harriet 18, 22
Munson, Audrey 31

National Velvet 152
Navarro, Ramon 56, 57
Nazimova, Alla 35, 40, 41, 55–7, 100
Negri, Pola 27
Nelson, Harmon 157–8
Night Gallery 81
Ninotchka 142
Nissen, Greta 84
Nolan, Mary 98–9
Normand, Mabel 26, 30, 33, 34, 70, 90, 108
North West Mounted Police 144
Novak, Kim 176–7

Oberon, Merle 27, 101–2
O'Brien, Margaret 27
Old Clothes 78
Olivier, Lawrence 200
O'Neill, Oona 146, 147
One Million Years BC 108
Open City 135

Pabst, Georg W 51–2
Pandora's Box 51
Parsons, Louella 68, 69
Pathé 23
Pavan, Marisa 175
Peck, Gregory 201
Peters, Jean 175
Pickford, Jack 44
Pickford, Mary 13, 26, 27, 28, 40, 44, 49, 56, 106
Pinky 131, 168
Platinum Blonde 87
Platt, Sylvia 137–8, 139
Porgy and Bess 170
Powell, Frank 31
Powell, William 91
Power, Tyrone 104, 132, 153, 182
Powers, Pat 39
Preminger, Otto 161, 167, 168, 169, 170, 177, 178
Preston, Robert 144
Prince Rainier 176
Private Life of Henry VIII, The 102
Purity 31
Purviance, Edna 33, 34, 70
Putti, Lya de 56

Queen Kelly 32

Rambova, Natascha 57
Ramona 148
Randall, Tony 166
Rapf, Harry 76, 77
Rappe, Virginia 53–4
Ray, Nicholas 80
Rear Window 176
Reckless 91
Reid, Wallace 71
Return of Frank James, The 153
Rice, Ella 154
Rich, Ruth 30
Rin-Tin-Tin 125
Roach, Hal 22, 84, 108, 143
Robin Hood 117
Rogers, Ginger 27, 149

Roland, Gilbert 59
Rooney, Mickey 92, 93, 133
Rossellini, Roberto 135–6
Rossen, Hal 91
Rubens, Alma 30, 71
Rutherford, Ann 92, 93
Russell, Jane 159, 171
Russell, William 123

Sadie Thompson 152
St Clair, Mal 124
Saint Joan, 178
Salome 152
Satterlee, Margaret 140
Scala, Gia 191
Scarface 155
Scarlet Empress, The 100
Schenck, Joe 102, 127, 143, 196–7
Schrock, Raymond 125
Schubert, J J 76
Schulberg, B P 48, 58, 60, 99
Seberg, Jean 178–9
Secret Six, The 86
Selig, William 24
Selznick, David O, 46, 82, 113, 114, 115, 117–21, 135, 161–5, 193, 214
Selznick, Lewis 33, 38–46, 106
Selznick, Myron 46, 116, 120
Sennett, Mack 21–2, 26, 29–30, 33, 69, 124
Serlin, Oscar 120
Seven Year Itch, The 172
Shanghai Express 100
Shearer, Norma 27, 116, 157
Sheehan, Winfield 147–8
Shepherd, Cybil 215
She Shows Him How 76
Signoret, Simone 201
Simmons, Jean 160–61
Sinatra, Frank 199, 210
Skouras, Spyrous 198
Smith, Chester Harvey 180–82
Snake Pit, The 131
Snider, Paul 215–16
Some Like it Hot 200

Something's Got to Give 205, 206, 207
Song of Bernadette, The 163
Sperling, Milton 109
Spielberg, Steven 81
Stallone, Sylvester 192, 217
Stanwyck, Barbara 27
Stardust 105
Sten, Anna 27
Sternberg, Josef Von 99–101
Stewart, James 132
Strangers on a Train 164
Stratton, Dorothy 215–16
Strawberry Blonde 149
Streisand, Barbra 217
Strickland, Howard 89–90
Stroheim, Erich von 32–3, 92, 98, 99, 182
Stromberg, Hunt 79
Stromboli 136
Sundown 153
Swanson, Gloria 27, 30, 204
Sweet, Blanche 13, 32, 49, 106

Talmadge, Constance 30, 40, 55
Talmadge, Norma 30, 40, 55
Tamango 170
Taylor, Elizabeth 161, 207
Taylor, Robert 132
Taylor, William Desmond 70–71, 90
Temple, Shirley 129–30
Teresa 175
Terry, Alice 56
Thalberg, Irving 48, 87, 89
Thaxter, Phyllis 162
Thomas, Olive 40, 41–7, 52, 56
Tierney, Gene 151, 152–3
Tobacco Road 153
To Catch a Thief 176
Tone, Franchot 76
Tonight and Every Night 150
Torch Song 80
Turner, Lana 27, 92, 157

Unconquered, The 145
Underwater 171
Underworld 99

Valentino, Rudolph 55, 56
Van Doren, Mamie 174–5
Vargas, Alberto 42
Varsity Show 109
Velez, Lupe 109–11
Velvet Lips 76
Vendetta 160

Walker, Phyllis *see* Jennifer Jones
Walker, Robert 162, 163–5
Walters, Charles 80
Wanger, Walter 50–51
Warner, Jack 48, 102, 127, 140
Wayne, John 59–60, 174, 179, 180–82
Wayward Bus, The 172
Wedding March 32
Weiger, Bella *see under* Darvi
Weinstein, Henry 207, 208
Weismuller, Johnny 110
Welles, Orson 150
West, Mae 95, 111
Whatever Happened To Baby Jane? 80
White, Loray 178
White, Pearl 56
Whitman, Stuart 170
Whitney, Jock 114, 115
Wilder, Billy 142
Wilding, Michael 161
Wild Party 85
Will Success Spoil Rock Hunter? 166, 172
Wings 84
Winters, Shelley 198
Withers, Jane 92
Wood, Natalie 191

Young, Clara Kimball 39–40, 55
Young, Loretta 27, 28, 116, 148, 169

Zanuck, Darryl 48–9, 55, 63–4, 87, 97, 103, 104–5, 122–31, 133, 148, 149, 151, 153, 163,

166, 168, 169, 182–3, 185–9, 190, 193, 198, 214, 215
Zanuck, Virginia *see under* Fox
Ziegfeld, Florenz 36, 41–2

Ziegfeld Follies, The 50, 69, 98, 143
Zinneman, Fred 175
Zukor, Adolph 54–5, 70–71, 90